THE ANCIENT 360 DAY YEAR

THE ANCIENT 360 DAY YEAR

WHAT IT WAS.... AND HOW IT CHANGED

DALE WONG

Advantage™

Copyright © 2006 by Dale Wong

All rights reserved. No part of this book may be used or reproduced in any manner whatsoever without prior written consent of the author, except as provided by the United States of America copyright law.

Published by Advantage, Charleston, South Carolina.
Member of Advantage Media Group.

ADVANTAGE is a registered trademark and the
Advantage colophon is a trademark of Advantage Media Group, Inc.

Printed in the United States of America

First Printing: August 2006
ISBN: 978-1-59932-013-7
Illustrations: Unless noted otherwise, Ms. Melanie R. Wong

Most Advantage Media Group titles are available at special quantity discounts for bulk purchases for sales promotions, premiums, fundraising, and educational use. Special versions or book excerpts can also be created to fit specific needs.

For more information, please write: Special Markets, Advantage Media Group, P.O. Box 272, Charleston, SC 29402 or call 1.866.775.1696.

FOREWORD

"At this time Hezekiah fell dangerously ill and the prophet Isaiah son of Amoz came to him and said, 'This is the word of the Lord: Give your last instructions to your household, for you are a dying man and will not recover.' Hezekiah turned his face to the wall and offered this prayer to the Lord: 'O Lord, remember how I have lived before thee, faithful and loyal in thy service, always doing what was good in thine eyes.' And he wept bitterly. The word of the Lord came to Isaiah 'Go and say to Hezekiah: "This is the word of the Lord the God of your father David: I have heard your prayers and seen your tears; I will add fifteen years to your life. I will deliver you and this city from the king of Assyria and will protect this city." Then Isaiah told them to apply a fig-plaster; so they made one and applied it to the boil, and he recovered. Then Hezekiah said, 'By what sign shall I know that I shall go up into the house of the Lord?" And Isaiah said, 'This shall be your sign from the Lord that he will do as He has promised. Watch the shadow cast by the sun on the stairway of Ahaz: I will bring backwards ten steps the shadow which has gone down on the stairway.' And the sun went back ten steps on the stairway down which it had gone." (Isaiah 38:1-8, New English Bible)

In a very strict sense, no part of the Bible can be correctly understood except in the context of the entire Book, and in the following technical study this might be especially true. The material necessarily deals with the intricate. It is exhaustive in its research, yet in its welcome uniqueness it becomes both thought provoking and highly stimulating in the presentation of its exciting ideas! To be fully appreciated, it must be read and understood in its relationship to a clearly stated, and by this time, a largely historic plan and purpose which God has with this earth. It stretches back to the Adamic creation and onward to a future time not yet disclosed. The described event, in the Scripture verses quoted above, may at first, seem isolated and in large measure irrelevant to the general concerns of professing Christians, but what was done and the effects which were thus precipitated have had a monumental effect on the time frame in which we have subsequently come to operate. We can, if we wish, dismiss the record of the shadow as it was brought back ten steps on the stairway of Ahaz, but we cannot deny the disruption which rendered the calendars at that time hopelessly obsolete.

By the time King Hezekiah reigned over the Kingdom of Judah the drama of God's relationship with His creation had covered over 3000 years. There had been a few bright spots, but for the most part, it had been a far cry from the potential good for which it had been created. At one point, what God had made was virtually destroyed and a new beginning revolved around one man and his family. Centuries later the Divine program was further developed when specific promises were made to Abraham concerning the Land of Caanan. He was told that he and his "seed" would inherit this land for an everlasting possession. Paul tells us these promises form the foundation of the Gospel message which must be believed and obeyed if salvation is to become possible. He further states that the "seed" promised referred to Jesus Christ.

Abraham's descendants migrated to Egypt where severe and prolonged famine had driven them. Over a period of 250 years they gradually multiplied and became a great nation. When they were brought up out of the land of Egypt they were given a Law at Mt. Sinai and eventually returned to reoccupy this very Land of Promise. It was, however, a continued story of unhappiness and disappointment. As a nation they seemed so unable to reap the tangible benefits which would be reasonably expected as a result of knowing and worshiping the only true and living God. The idol-worship of the surrounding nations proved to be an irresistible attraction, and as predicted, led to intolerable conditions which would not be allowed to continue.

Prophets were sent repeatedly to reprove and to warn them of the dire consequences which would attend their disobedience. There were no ears to hear and no heart to turn toward the righteousness and purity enjoined upon them. As a result the tragedies of destruction and captivity were eminent. The Assyrians (700 B.C.) were successful in their campaign against the Ten Tribes of Israel located in the Northern part of the Kingdom. Cities were destroyed, men, women and children slaughtered, and the remaining survivors summarily dispersed as slaves into the vast regions of the Empire.

A hundred years would pass, and now it was Judah's turn. The brave reforms of Hezekiah had brought about a mere surface change in the behavior of the people. True, the Assyrians in their intended assault against Jerusalem, had been destroyed, but in the fifteen years that had been added to Hezekiah's life, Manasseh his son was born. It was this dreadful tyrant who led Judah into the lowest depths of moral and religious degradation. Now the clouds of impending disaster hung over Jerusalem as the invaders from Babylon assembled their plundering armies and moved relentlessly towards them. The horrors of the siege cannot be imagined. Seventy years of captivity would pass before they were permitted to return to their land and repair the ruins of their city.

This study undertakes the somewhat tedious and difficult task of helping us to understand the phenomenon of the retrogressing shadow which, with the setting sun, had already gone down ten steps on the stairway of Ahaz. Until this time the movements of the sun, the moon and the earth had been in perfect harmony. Discovered calendars from civilizations around the world universally reckoned the year as consisting of 360 days, with 12 months of 30 days each. It was around this precise system of time-management that the main features of Israel's religious observances were centered.

Now Hezekiah was instructed to watch the shadow on the sun dial as it reversed its direction and slowly returned to the top of the stairs [one possible interpretation of the nature of the sundial – DWW]. Since the time that shadow returned, things have never been the same. Calendars the world over had to be revised to accommodate a longer and more awkward period of time which the earth, traveling at 66,600 miles per hour, took to make its journey around the sun. The best that could be done to manage the 365.25 day year was to devise a calendar which had 12 months of differing lengths, some 30 days, some 31, and then set aside a month with only 28 days. To this month an extra day had to be added every four years to keep the time-measurement from running behind. In addition, the moon, instead of its former 30-day regularity, was also affected. Its cycle was altered to approximately 29.5 days and its usefulness as a device for measuring time became far more complicated.

The reader is invited to carefully consider the material which has taken over ten years to assemble and meticulously verify. It essentially describes the extent to which our Almighty God is prepared to manifest His power and control. It assured King Hezekiah that he would continue his recovery and go up to the house of the Lord to worship, but it also set before the world an undeniable witness to symbolize the continuing disharmony between His throne in the heavens and a capricious creation on the earth beneath. Perhaps for some, it may take considerable fortitude to set aside the discredits heaped upon the Bible by scientific thought. Admittedly, the ideas of atheistic educators and the discordant jumble of established Christian thinking make the private investigations of those who try "to make sense" of what the Bible is telling us, a difficult and formidable undertaking. It is hoped that this study will encourage a determined effort to discover the true message of the Bible. It is God's invitation to become part of His original intention that the earth will one day be filled with His glory!

Perhaps there will be a day, sometime soon, when the harmony between the sun, moon, and the earth will be restored, and thus reflect the peace of the coming age when God's will is done here on this earth as it is now done in heaven.

Mr. Thomas Mitchell

CONTENTS

INTRODUCTION

This book identifies and then describes a miracle. It is not a visible miracle, recorded in Holy Scripture to lay a foundation for faith in God's invisible power. This miracle cannot be explained by natural causes yet has been with us for 2,700 years, observable by all people of the Earth. There can be no doubt that its discovery was intended for this generation.

We live in an age when "miracles" are justified by science. A miracle not of scientific origins is almost always greeted with skepticism. Science has successfully wrested control of men's faith. Jesus faced a generation of faithless people seeking a sign from him. His reply was, ***"An evil and adulterous generation seeks after a sign, and no sign will be given to it except the sign of the prophet Jonah."*** (Matthew 12:31). That miracle, Jonah kept alive in the belly of a great fish for three days, prefigured a time when Jesus would die, be buried for three days, and emerge reborn in spirit nature. It showed the way that men could save themselves. But Jesus' resurrection cannot be proven by scientific methods, only through circumstantial evidence.

This miracle occurred in the distant past in the land of the tribe of Judah of the divided kingdom of Israel. It happened during the reign of King Hezekiah and the prophet Isaiah. The circumstance of the miracle can be read in the Bible, in the books of the Kings (2 Kings 20), the Chronicles (2 Chronicles 32) and the prophet Isaiah (Isaiah 38). Prior to this time the world's civilizations all used a year consisting of 360 days. Suddenly a new year emerged consisting of about 365¼ days. Similarly a complete lunar cycle was recorded as taking 30 days. The new and present lunar cycle consists of a little more than 29½ days. Ancient people with an imperfect understanding of the cosmos struggled to explain this new situation. A sample from the Roman historian Plutarch: "*Hermes played at draughts with the moon, won from her the seventieth part of each of her periods of illumination, and from all the winnings composed five days, and intercalated them as an addition to the 360 days*." The book shows the connection between the miracle shown to Hezekiah and this change in the length of the month and year. The cause of this change is of Divine origin and must be accepted as such. The effect is simulated using well-established physical and mathematical principles of celestial mechanics.

The earlier chapters of the book serve to prepare the reader for understanding later chapters. No prior understanding of astronomy, calendars or the Bible is required but some understanding of any of these three subjects will enhance the reader's appreciation. Detailed discussion of physics, mathematics and other subjects are left to the appendices for the reader who wishes to obtain a substantial understanding of the subject matter. Chapter 1 takes the reader to the very beginning by considering the matter of what time is and how it is classified. It is important to understand how ancient people viewed astronomical events and how they grouped them into days, months and years. We then take advantage of our modern understanding of time events. Chapter 2 deals with the subject of calendars. Taking what has been learned in Chapter 1, the reader now learns how a calendar is constructed to order the chronological events of human life. The art of modern calendar making is explored from the historical perspective of ancient Babylon through to the methods of the churches of Christendom. Chapter 3 is a "fork in the road" on our journey. A consideration of orbital motion from the perspective of the physicist is given. This is necessary to prepare the reader for understanding the extraordinary events of the miracle shown on the sundial of Ahaz as a sign to King Hezekiah. Time is taken to discuss the subject of Divine intervention on the natural laws of the universe. This is necessary for two reasons: to acquaint the reader with the principles of the subject and to answer the inevitable critics that demand a mechanistic explanation for everything. Chapter 4 builds the case for an ancient 360-Day year. Evidence from the Bible and the astronomical observations and calendars of ancient civilizations prior to the 7th century B. C. is provided. The reader will need the understanding he has gleaned from the prior three chapters to obtain the benefit of this chapter. Having obtained a solid foundation for the 360-Day year, and the astronomical characteristics of it, we move onto a chronological dissertation of King Hezekiah, the miracle and its place in God's own time measurement of the affairs of man in Chapter 5. Chapter 6 is a discussion of the significance of the miracle.

This book will affirm and deepen the faith of Jews and Christians. They will be awed by God's power and wisdom and intrigued by the significance of the event in a wider spiritual context. The miracle begs the question "*Why?*" and while the book delves into this it is left to others to more completely answer the question. To non-believers the miracle is both a rose and a thorn. A thorn because such overwhelming evidence of the existence of an omniscient, omnipotent, and omnipresent God demands a considered response. A rose because the now revealed beauty and majesty of this stunning miracle may stimulate them to invite God into his own life.

"And God said, Let there be lights in the firmament of the heaven to divide the day from the night; and let them be for signs, and for seasons, and for days, and years:"

(Genesis 1:14)

What is Time?

Time is the structure within which God works His plan for the Earth. But answering the question, "*What is Time*?" from a *physical* point of view is not as simple as it might at first appear. Time to most of us has become such an intimate part of our existence and we are so used to using it, we may underestimate its underlying significance. In fact, if you consider the matter a little more deeply, you will discover that it isn't easily defined. For example, a stranger on the street asks us, "*What time is it*?" Our reply might typically be, "*12:45*" or "*A quarter to 1*" or "*15 minutes to 1.*" What we are saying is that "*I observe the hands of the clock in a certain position*," or "*I see the numbers '1,' '2,' '4' and '5' and this means a certain moment of the day.*" We are making an observation and describing a point in a series of events. The events are the issues of our life. Scientists refer to the event point as an *epoch*, an instant in time. In a sense, time is a reference frame in which a continuous stream of events is measured using epochs.

For example, assume you are painting a fence. You get in a rhythm of moving your paintbrush up and down as you apply the paint to the fence. You might say that painting one-half of the length of the fence requires 500 strokes of the brush. Each stroke of the brush represents a unit of time. Later, you may wash your car. It requires the equivalent of 266¼ strokes of the paintbrush to complete. It is apparent that time is the description of one event in the reference frame of another. In this case, the event described is washing a car. It is described in the reference frame of brush strokes, an event having certain duration. The first instant of the brush touching the wood can be called the *opening* or *first* epoch. The instant when the brush is lifted off the wood is called the *closing* or *last* epoch. The stream of time between these two epochs can be called the *time event*[1ℵ].

While the use of paintbrush strokes is an acceptable time event, certain demands are placed on a useful time system for civil purposes:

1. **Regularity** – However slight the differences in paintbrush strokes might be, when we begin to break the event down into smaller and smaller fractions, we would discover unpredictable variations in the length of the event. We say that the time event is *irregular*. Regularity is an important requirement of a useful time system.
2. **Observability** – While the fence painting time system may be locally useful, it is probably not useful to anyone else. The time-system event must be widely observable.
3. **Repeatability** – While this may appear to be the same as regularity, for time systems, it is quite different. Repeatability is concerned with cycles of time events. This is important when we consider biblical time, which is principally concerned with the relationship between the cycles of the Moon and the Sun.

It is intuitively obvious that the motion of the heavenly bodies adheres to all of these demands. While other time systems are created for various purposes, the sun, moon and stars are the only truly useful time systems for a world of people. Human life is so governed by them and our activities on the Earth are so greatly influenced by them (day and night, seasons) that it is perfectly natural that we will always resort to their use as our time system of choice. For the believer in God's word, Genesis 1:14 is sufficiently complete that we should look to no other time system than the motion of the heavenly

1 ℵ "Any repetitive phenomenon whatever, the recurrences of which can be counted, is a measure of time." G. M. Clemence[1]

bodies as the only time system of interest. This will be the position taken for the remainder of the book.

As previously discussed, all of these time events involve cycles; the opening and closing epoch are represented by the return of the heavenly body to the same location in space. The astronomical methods of the ancient people always involved observation of repetition of these cycles. The *day* time event is, approximately, the return of the Sun to the same position on the horizon. A *year* time event is when the Sun returns to the exact same position in the sky. A *month* time event is the observance the return of the waning and waxing Moon to its original appearance or *phase*. It is not necessary to know anything about these cycles to be able to use them. In God's infinite wisdom, He has placed these heavenly bodies in the sky to allow people of all generations to measure the events of their life, their communities and their civilizations by the recurrent cycles of the sun, moon, and stars.

Ancient people used the *angles only* method to determine their time systems. They measured the angle of a celestial body relative to markers they observed from earth. While there is some evidence that certain ancient astronomers had a primitive notion of the distance separating their position to a heavenly body, it never found its place in the astronomy of any of the important civilizations until the sixteenth century A. D. It was Johannes Kepler who first described, mathematically, the principles of orbital motion of the planets. It was Isaac Newton who introduced the laws of gravity to the world to explain the physical principles of why the planets orbit the Sun. It then became possible to include the distance between the earth, moon, and sun to create new mathematical rules to establish a connection between time and characteristics of an orbit. It is the concept of distance between heavenly bodies that ancient people did not understand and it this understanding that separates ancient and modern astronomy.

Naked Eye Astronomy

Civil time systems are based on the movement of heavenly bodies. Ancient civilizations employed numerous (clever) methods for measuring time from direct observation. The techniques used by ancient astronomers are sometimes collectively referred to as *naked eye astronomy*. The obvious reason for this name is that it is astronomy without the benefit of sophisticated, modern instruments (like telescopes, radar, lasers, etc.). There is a tendency for Bible students to rush into a study of biblical time systems without benefit of a basic understanding of how ancient people viewed the movement of the ***lights in the firmament of the heaven*** across the sky. Usually this study begins with a tour of biblical calendars and the student tries to understand time systems through complex explanations about intercalation, rectification of the seasons, lunisolar transformations, etc. There is a resulting tendency to underestimate the ancient astronomers' ability to make precise time calculations. Perhaps it is our own tendency in our sophistry to presume that science and mathematics can answer all questions and that anything that does not conform to its strict edicts must be regarded as nonsensical and even heretical. Authoritative investigators of the astronomical techniques used by the ancient scientists often have the opposite view. They find that the ancient methods of time measurement were quite effective and often express surprise at the sophistication of their approach and the high precision they obtained.

Our approach to introducing the topic of ancient and modern astronomy will be from the point of view of the observer on earth. This was the only perspective understood by ancient people. We will begin by assuming that we know nothing about modern astronomical principles. What this means, practically, is that we assume that the observer has no idea of the distance from their position to the celestial bodies. Students of ancient astronomy have long benefited from an introduction to astronomical concepts and our introduction should also be viewed as essential to understanding the subject matter. Our imaginary guide will be an ancient astronomer; perhaps we could even imagine the prophet Isaiah as our guide. However, it is not necessary that we pretend we are in ancient Judah. We could just as easily be in Africa, Asia, Europe or North America with little variation in what will be described.

The Night Sky in Ancient Judah

Our tour begins with us standing alone with our guide. Pretend you are standing somewhere in ancient Judah, as it is the focus of the investigations of this book. It is the seventh century B. C. It is night and we are fortunate that there is a cloudless sky. The sky over our head appears like an enormous canopy with holes of light. Over time we notice that the lights seem to move smoothly and slowly across the canopy. Collections of lights appear to trace out the shapes of animals, men, chariots, etc.; shapes that we are familiar with on earth. We notice that they always appear to keep the same relative distance to each other. Our guide points to certain lights that are low in the sky, barely above the horizon. He tells us that if we were to keep watching the lights they would rise over our heads and set on the other side of the canopy. We notice that some stars rise over certain hills that are familiar to us, others seem to rise out of valleys. We recognize the faint outline of these traces and know that beyond them are the lands of the ten tribes of Israel. To the east is the Great Sea, in the opposite direction is the Salt Sea. Farther along the horizon it is *mid-bawr'* "the wilderness" where the Israelites wandered for forty years. Farther still are the Nile and Egypt. From this we have a sense of our orientation. By fixing on one spot on the horizon we can see where all of the lights are relative to this spot. We sense a change in relative distance as an angle along the ground and an angle in the sky above the horizon. This view, our guide tells us, is the horizon view.

"Look towards Israel," our guide tells us. In the sky is one point in the midst of a group of lights that all of the lights seem to rotate around. "*That is tsaw-fone', due north,*" explains our guide. We have found our first true direction. We note the point on the horizon, the exact location of true north. We turn to the right, one-quarter of the circle of the horizon, and our guide tells us, "*This is keh'-dem, east, the place of the rising of sheh'-mesh, the sun*". Directly opposite to north is *neh'-gheb* south, directly opposite to east is *yawm*, west.

Certain lights in the sky are much larger and brighter than the other lights. "*That is yaw-ray'-akh, the moon. Yahweh has told us to use it to measure the beginning of our months*" our guide explains. "*Every 30 days, yome, the moon looks the same.*" It is dark, a crescent shape, half-light, full-light, and so on. "*We do not know why*," explains our guide, "*it is the way Yahweh has made it.*" Our guide points to other bright lights in the sky; one blinking red, one green, others white. "*They are the maz-zaw-law', the planets. They all follow an arc in the southern sky.*" Our guide explains that they do not move in the same way and at the same speed as the rest of the lights. They are special. The moon and the planets follow the same line always. Our night's work is over. Our guide advises us to rest and bids us farewell, and we sleep until morning.

The Day Sky in Ancient Judah

We meet our guide in the morning, just before the time when the sun appears on the horizon. "*It always shows up in the east*," says the guide. In the ground are two, large stakes with forks in their tops. A large distance, 200 cubits, separates them. "*Line up the forks at the top of the stakes with your eyes. We use them to determine the length of the shaw-neh', a cycle or year.*"

Looking along the stakes we see that the sun is off to the left of the line of the forks. "*It is not yet the closing of a year*," says the guide. The guide explains that when the sun is directly along the line of the stakes, it is due east. "*Also, the day and the night are exactly the same length of time when this happens.*" The guide tells us that this occurs at only two times in the year. The number of days that separates them is exactly 180 days. "*The sun is due east on the 15th day in the beginning of months – the month Abib – and once in the end of the year – on the 15th day of the month Ethanim.*" Throughout the year, the sun appears to the left of the stake and seems to hang there for many days when it is farthest to the left of the line of stakes. "*In the time of the year when the sun moves higher in the sky, the day lasts much longer than the night.*

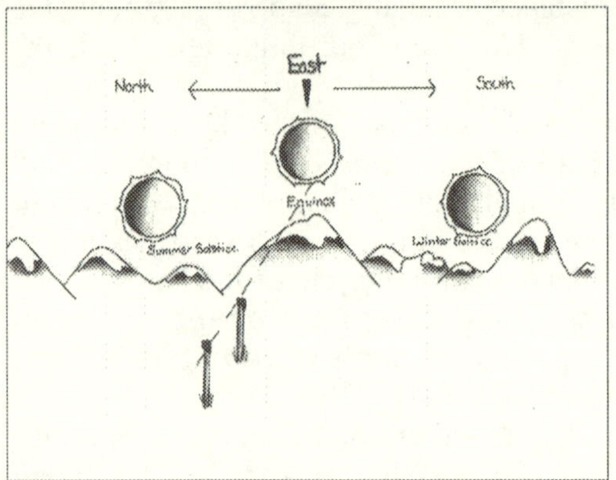

When the Sun moves to the south, the days are much shorter. When the Sun is north of the stakes, it moves from the month Ethanim into the winter. When it returns to the stake line, it passes through Abib and then moves south as summer comes." The guide explains that it never changes this movement. "*We do not know why it does this*," explains the guide. "*We only know that God has shown us that when the Sun is lined up through the forks of the stakes and when the day and the night are of equal length, it is the end of the year (Exodus 23:16). We also know that it is the time to celebrate skenopegia, the feast of ingathering, at this time.*" The guide further explains the same thing occurs in the month Abib except that it will then be the time of the feast of unleavened bread and the keeping of *pas'-khah*, the Passover. He mentions in passing that when the sun is lined up with the stakes the moon is full when it appears on the horizon.

Our guide tells us that we need know nothing more to make a perfectly adequate calendar. Time between months and years is made up of a simple count of days. The day is broken up into portions called *watches*. Some, the affluent, use a sundial with lines to determine the parts of the day. But this is not necessary to make a calendar. He says good-bye and heads back to Jerusalem to complete his priestly duties.

Almost everyone can understand what has just been described. It requires virtually no understanding whatsoever of anything astronomical. Common sense and a little ingenuity that could easily be learned and passed on to succeeding generations alone are required. Kingdoms throughout the Earth would readily develop similar methods for measuring time. Historical records show that this is indeed the case. Astronomers would refine these methods and very precise time calculations would result. However, as we will see in a later chapter, previous to about 700 B. C., these civilizations had a 360-day year and not a 365¼-day year. They had a 30-day month and not a 29.53095-day month as we presently have. They did not insert seconds, minutes, hours, days or months into their calendar to "correct" them. They did not adjust the solar time to match lunar time or even star time (referred to as *sidereal time*). The lights in the heaven were all in sync and converting between one and another time system was accomplished with simple addition or subtraction of days.

Our imaginary guide in Judah was leading us through what we would have observed in a 360-Day year consisting of 12 months of 30 days. It is not what is observed today, although almost all of the guide's advice can be followed in our modern times. In subsequent sections we will describe the variations necessary to accommodate a modern view of the skies over ancient Judah or Israel.

The Present Day and Night Sky in Judah

In order for our imaginary tour to agree with the present situation in the day and night sky over Judah, we would need to adjust some things. First, the Hebrew months Abib and Ethanim are still roughly the equivalent of our March and September months, respectively. Their names were changed to Nisan and Tisri after the exile of the Jews to Babylon. However, dating Jewish feasts is more complex. The New Moon in these months may be found to occur anytime from September 5th to October 5th. Here are the results for the spring and fall appearance of the New Moon and the Full Moon that follows for A.D. 1999–2004 in Israel:

New Moon				Full Moon			
Spring		Fall		Spring		Fall	
Month	Day	Month	Day	Month	Day	Month	Day
March	17	September	9	March	31	September	25
March	6	September	27	March	20	October	13
March	25	September	17	April	8	October	2
March	14	September	7	March	28	September	21
April	1	September	26	April	16	October	10
March	20	September	14	April	5	September	28

There is no obvious relationship between the lunar and solar time systems. Presently, the equinox occurs on March 21 and September 23 in our calendar and has changed position in the calendar very little over the centuries. Were our guide to try to explain to us the relationship between the spring and fall appearance of the New Moon and the equinoxes, it would not be simple.

This "confusion" in the calendar apparently did not occur in distant ancient times (prior to the seventh century B. C.). We will leave a detailed account of the calendar for a later chapter. Let us now switch to a modern view of calendars and astronomy.

Modern Astronomy

Celestial bodies provide the standards for determining the periods of a calendar. This is why the study of the celestial bodies is of premier importance and must be understood *first* before considering calendars. Consequently, we will not consider calendars until a later chapter.

The principles of modern astronomy help us explain what the ancient people saw. The primary difference between the older, naked eye astronomy and the newer, modern astronomy is the understanding of distance between celestial objects. Ancient people did not know how far away the moon, the sun or the stars actually were. They saw angles, relative distances of the lights to landmarks they were familiar with. Some civilizations had instruments for more precise measurement, some employed methods such as the sighting sticks discussed in the previous section to determine the length of the year. Now, for celestial bodies in the solar system, we have a very good idea of the true distance between bodies. Modern space travel and the placement of satellites demand high precision work in the study of their orbital motion. The equations of motion due to mutual gravitation have been in use for over 300 years with high precision.

The Solar System

The solar system is comprised of eight major planets. Pluto's erratic motion – formerly the ninth planet – has forced astronomers to rethink its position as a major planet and, at the time of writing, it has been downgraded to a minor planet. Many satellites (moons) orbit these major planets. Asteroids, comets, meteroids, dust and gases make up the remainder of the mass in the solar system. The Sun dominates the solar system and all of the mass in the solar system orbits the sun. The reason for this is due to an effect called gravitation. The strength of gravitational forces is proportional to the mass of the celestial body. For example, the sun's volume is 1,303,000 times that of Earth and contains 99.8 percent of the solar system's mass. The gravitational force exerted by the sun on a comet is much greater than the gravitational force exerted by the comet on the sun. Strictly speaking, planets do not orbit around the sun but actually orbit around the *barycenter* of the solar system. This is the center of mass of the solar system. However, to high precision, the center of the sun can be assumed to be the center of mass of the solar system. An orbital system based on using the center of the sun is called a *heliocentric system*.

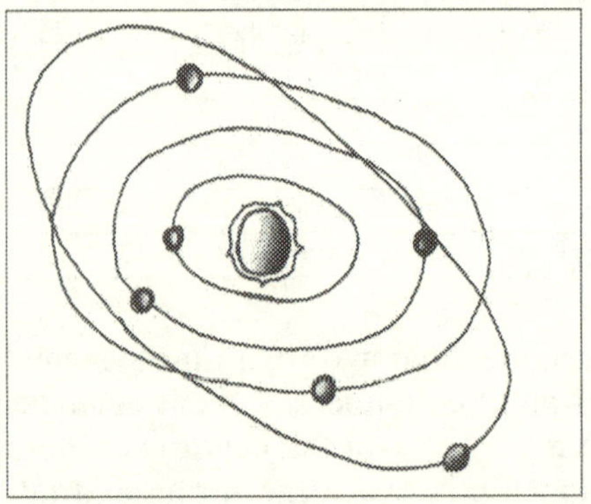

Ancient people knew of seven planets in our solar system. The root meaning of the word *planet* is *wanderer*. The planets were confusing to them due to their erratic motion in the skies over the period of a year as they appeared to wander relative to the stars. This confusion was due to the difference between the different orbits of inferior and superior planets. Inferior planets have orbits inside the earth's orbit and superior planets are outside of the earth's orbit. The Bible mentions some planets but never indicates that their motion is of interest as a time system.

Orbital Characteristics of the Planets

The earth has a mean distance from the sun of approximately 149,600,000 km. This distance is referred to as an *astronomical unit* of distance or "A. U." Mercury–closest to the sun–has a mean distance of 0.39 A. U. whereas Neptune has a distance of 30.06 A. U. The distance from the sun varies throughout the annual orbit of all of the planets around the sun. Modern planetary orbits occur along an oval curve called an *ellipse*. The sun is situated at one of the foci of the ellipse. Elliptical orbits that are increasingly elongated are referred to as having a higher orbital *eccentricity*. An orbital eccentricity of 0 is a circle. An orbital eccentricity of 1 is a straight line. The table below shows some of the basic elements of the eight planets and the moon:

Name	Equatorial Diameter (km)	Mass (kg)	Semi-Major Axis (A.U.)	Sidereal Orbital Period (days)	Eccentricity (e)
Sun	1,392,000	1.9891×10^{30}	0	0	0
Moon	3,476.2	7.347673×10^{22}	0.0026	27.32166155	0.0554900489
Mercury	4,879.4	3.302×10^{23}	0.38709893	87.96935	0.20563069
Venus	12,103.7	4.8685×10^{24}	0.72333199	224.70096	0.00677323
Earth	12,756.28	5.9736×10^{24}	1.00000011	365.25696	0.01671022
Mars	6,804.9	6.4185×10^{24}	1.52366231	686.9601	0.09341233
Jupiter	142,984	1.899×10^{27}	5.20336301	4,335.3545	0.04839266
Saturn	120,536	5.6846×10^{26}	9.53707032	10,757.7365	0.05415060
Uranus	51,118	8.6832×10^{25}	19.19126393	30,685.00	0.04716771
Neptune	49,528	1.0243×10^{26}	30.06896348	60,190.00	0.00858587

It can be clearly seen that the orbits of the planets are all very nearly circles. The exception to this rule is Mercury. Comets are an example of a type of celestial object with a highly eccentric orbit. The rate at which the planet orbits the sun is affected by its orbital eccentricity. When the planet is near the sun, gravitational forces cause it to be pulled more strongly. The planetary speed increases and a greater orbital distance is covered for a given unit of time (for example, over the period of a day). Farther away from the sun the planet slows as the sun's gravity is less strong and the orbital distance covered is less for a given unit of time. The mathematical consequences of these effects are discussed under Kepler's laws in a later chapter.

The planets, peculiarly, orbit the sun on a level plane referred to as *the ecliptic*. The ecliptic is an important reference frame that will be frequently referred to later in the book.

While the sun has an overwhelming gravitational influence on the planets, planets also attract each other. The gravitational forces are proportional to the *square of the distance* or *distance x distance*. This is why the stars do not have any noticeable effect on the orbits of individual planets. While they are no doubt massive, they are so far away their gravitational influence is minimal. The mutual gravitation of the planets is called *planetary aberration*. Celestial mechanics refers to the variable gravitational tugs by other planets as a *perturbation*. In precision calculation of orbital motion, these effects must be considered. In some cases, the center of gravity–the orbital barycenter–can be used with high precision and other perturbations can be ignored to a certain order of precision. This is often the case in modeling the motion of the earth-moon orbit around the sun. It has been shown that this is reasonable to a high degree of precision (see, for example, Brouwer and Clemence[2]) for short periods of time and under certain other conditions.

Modern Interpretation of the Relative Motion of the Sun

The daily and annual motion of the sun in the sky must have been confusing to ancient people. The diagram shows that the sun makes a "corkscrew" motion across the sky throughout the year. Now let's put the whole picture together using our modern understanding of celestial mechanics to aid our understanding of the yearly motion of the sun.

The Celestial Sphere

The diagram shows the apparent orbit of the sun around the earth throughout the year. It is referred to as the celestial sphere.

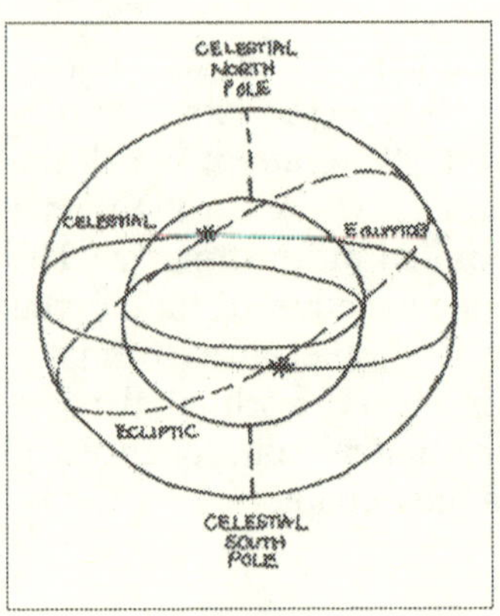

The celestial sphere has a northerly location of the axis or rotation of the earth called the *North Celestial Pole* or NCP. The equator is the celestial equator. A meridian line runs along the celestial sphere between the north celestial pole and the south celestial pole. This meridian is called the *prime meridian*. The celestial equator is very close to the earth's true equator and the prime meridian is 0° longitude (located at Greenwich, England, situated just east of London). If you traced the sun's position at noon each day throughout the year, it would follow a curve along the celestial sphere called *the ecliptic.* The daily motion of the sun is approximately parallel to the celestial equator. This apparent motion is caused by the rotation of the earth on its own axis. At the moment when the sun's apparent motion is on the celestial equator, the equinox occurs. This, as has been already stated, is the true beginning and ending of the year in the Bible. This occurs twice per year. In the spring, it is called the *vernal equinox.* In ancient Israel, it occurred during the month Abib (after the exile into Babylon, this month followed the Babylonian month naming convention Nisan). On the opposite side of the celestial equator, the month was named Ethanim (later, the Babylonian month name Tisri was adopted). Recall that the equinox meant to ancient people that the night and day were of an equal period of time. This is true everywhere on the earth.

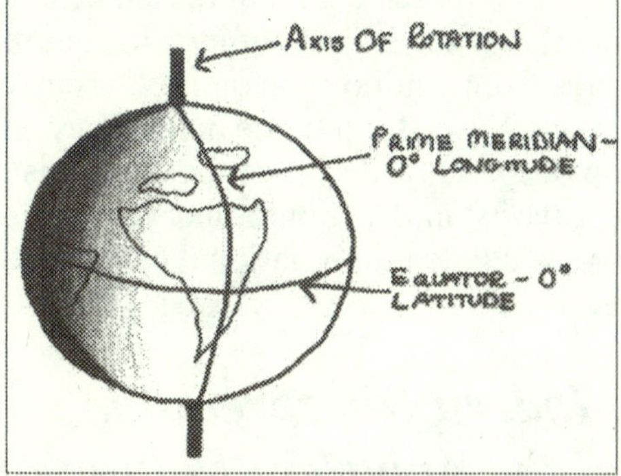

The Horizon View

An observer on earth sees the apparent movement of the sun from what astronomers refer to as a geocentric perspective. For him, the earth is flat. The line that separates sky from ground is called the *horizon.* Directly above him is the *zenith.* Directly below him is called the *nadir.* The day is separated from night by the appearance (or "rising") or disappearance (or "setting") of the sun on the horizon. The sun rises exactly in the east and sets exactly in the west at the equinoctial points. The end of the year, as it was indicated in Exodus, was at the fall equinox, in our present calendar around September 23rd. As the days go by, the sun rises further to the south and has a lower trajectory across the sky, lower to the horizon. At its lowest point in the sky, the day is the shortest. Presently, this occurs around December 22nd. This is termed the *winter solstice.* While this can be used as a possible beginning of the year, it was almost never used for that because the sun is known to *stand still* around this time. This makes precision, year-length determination very difficult. As winter proceeds and spring approaches, the sun *corkscrews* higher in the sky and once again we have another equinox: the *vernal* or *spring equinox.* This occurs at March 21st in the modern calendar. Later in the year, in the summer time, the Sun

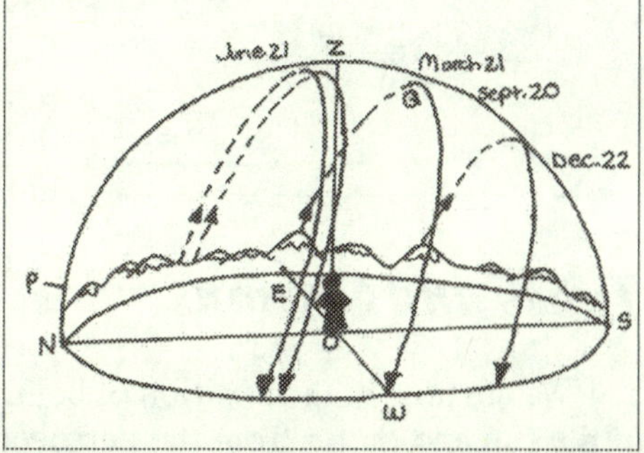

is the farthest north that it can appear and is highest in the sky. This is the summer solstice. The sun then "corkscrews" southward again. This is the cycle that ancient man used to determine the length of the year.

It is nonsensical that these ancient cultures could not accurately count the number of days from equinox to equinox. These ancient kingdoms counted 180 days from equinox to equinox. They could easily count 30 days in the period of one New Moon to the next. They easily knew that 12 of these periods made up one year. The tilt of the earth ensured that the changing seasons enforced regularity in the month and year count. It is not possible that they so badly miscalculated their national calendars that they would be out by 5¼ days ever year.

Modern Interpretation of the Apparent Motion of the Moon

If the sun was confusing to ancient people, surely the moon's appearance was even more confusing. The cyclic phases of the moon result from exposure of the earth-based observer to different percentages of the sunlit portion of the moon. In modern times, the cycle is completed in about 29½ days. The diagram shows clearly the circuit of the moon around the earth. The phases are all shown in the diagram. The Jews measured their months from New Moon to New Moon. Over a short period of the year, the differences between the present 29½-day month would so obviously be different from a 30-day month. The reader should refer to the appendix for a more detailed discussion of the orbital mechanics of the moon.

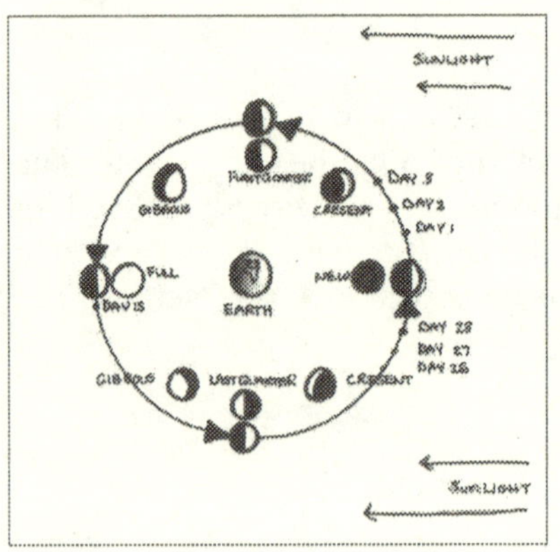

Times and Seasons

We are now in the position of being able to understand the apparent motion of the sun and moon from the perspective of both modern and ancient people. In this section, we focus on those astronomical aspects that will affect our understanding of biblical time systems.

The Day

The period of rotation of the earth once on its axis is called the day. In the Old Testament it is *yome* and in the New Testament it is referred to as *hay-mer'-ah*. It is also the period of light between sunrise and sunset. A simple addition of days can be used to keep time accurately. The day is the fundamental unit of time in civil timekeeping and in the Bible. Ancient people could not observe the earth rotating on its axis so instead they noted that the stars and the sun passed a certain point on the horizon, perhaps a landmark.

For modern purposes, where precise timekeeping is required, it has been noted that the earth's rotation irregularly accelerates and decelerates by a very small amount. It is also known to be slowing down by a small amount over a long period of time. The reader is directed to the appendices for a more detailed discussion of the measuring of the day.

There is no evidence that the rotation of the earth has ever experienced large changes in angular velocity (except perhaps the *long day* recorded in Joshua 10). We will assume throughout the investigations of this book that this is true.

We mention in passing that the day is divided into periods called hours. In the Old Testament they were referred to as *shaw-aw'*. Interestingly, this term is found only in the Aramaic text of Daniel. In the Greek New Testament it was *ho'-rah*, the twelfth part of the day. The principle purpose of the hour to ancient people was to divide the day along lines referred to as hour angles. When the sun or the stars or planets moved across the sky overhead, their transit passed equally-spaced marks and would *mark out* the hours of the day. One particular use of this was in the construction of sundials where hour lines would record the apparent daily motion of the Sun. It is an interesting and important fact that many ancient civilizations divided the resulting circle into 360 degrees, 1 degree for every day of the year. Bullinger[2] makes an interesting observation in this regard: "*No one can tell us why the number of degrees was first fixed at 360. It has come down to us from ancient times, and is used universally without question. It is this division of the Zodiac which gives the 12 months of the Zodiacal year. This is called the Prophetic year, for it is the year which is used in the prophecies of the Bible*." Such a designation easily points to a 360-day year, 1° for every day. Divisions by 30 days in a month lead to the number 12. This is the number of hours in the day and the number of hours in the night. Of course the use of degrees still persists in modern times with 15 degrees representing one hour of the day.

The Tilt of the Earth's Axis–The Lengthening and Shortening of the Day and the Seasons

Apart from the rotation of the Earth, no astronomical feature affects life on earth more than the tilt of the earth's axis. The tilt is presently at 23°27'. The diagram shows that the earth's northern hemisphere is tilted away from the sun during our winter months and tilted toward the sun during the summer months. The tilt governs the seasons and causes the fall, winter, spring, and summer cycles throughout the years. The occurrence of the seasons enforces calendar uniformity, as errors in matching the seasons in the year with a chosen calendar will eventually cause the months to be out of sync with the seasons. The Hebrew calendar has always related agricultural and festival occurrences–seasonal events–with a particular month and a particular time of the year. As we see later, this is especially important in the investigation of the ancient 360-day year.

The other effect of the tilt of the earth was on the arc of the sun's daily motion across the sky. This has already been discussed.

The Yearly Orbit of the Earth around the Sun

As the earth orbits the sun throughout the year, it changes its distance between them. The present 365¼-day orbit is referred to as an elliptical orbit. An exaggerated scale elliptical orbit is shown in the figure. The sun occupies one of the foci of the ellipse. The details of the configuration are left to a later chapter. The consequence is that the earth's motion around the sun is slowed during summer months (winter in the southern hemisphere) when it is furthest away from the sun and its velocity is the greatest when it is closest in early January (in the northern hemisphere). The point where the earth is closest to the sun is called perihelion and furthest is called aphelion.

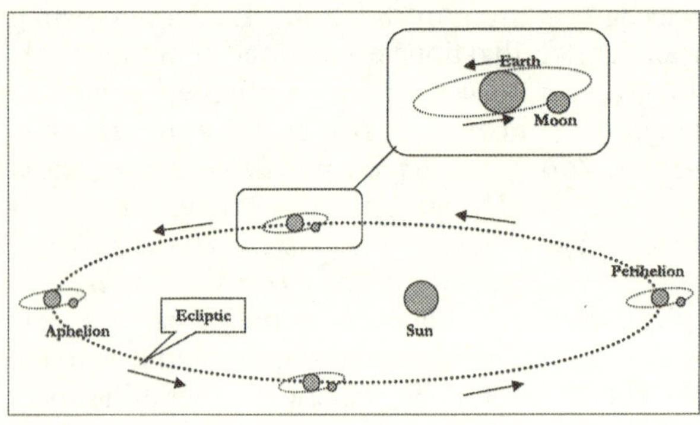

The plane on which the orbit of the earth around the sun occurs is called the ecliptic. The ecliptic appears to us in the northern hemisphere as an arc in the southern sky which the sun, moon and planets appear to move along throughout the year. From the preceding discussion, it is apparent that the earth's tilt is 23°27' removed from the plane of the ecliptic. When the sun's course strikes the exact location of the vertex where the tilt and the ecliptic arcs meet, this is called the equinox. The equinoxes were almost always the point at which ancient people began their New Year's Day. There are two equinoxes; the vernal (spring) equinox and the autumnal (fall) equinox.

Ancient people, of course, did not know about the motion of the earth around the sun. Nevertheless, the equinoxes were obvious points to mark the year because, (1) The time period of day and night were equal at the equinox; (2) the sun would rise in exactly the east and set exactly in the west at the equinox; (3) the change in the location of the sun's rising and setting is at its greatest at the time of the equinox (making it easiest to accurately pick the moment of the equinox and hence New Year's Day). Ancient people rarely picked the solstices for their New Year's Day because the sun "slows" in the sky making accurate picking of the New Year's Day more difficult. There does not appear to be a favored equinox as New Year's Day; both the vernal and autumnal equinox served as New Year's Day. For ancient Israel, the autumnal equinox was the beginning of their civil year and is referred to as the year's "closing."

Conjunction of the Sun, Moon and Earth– The New Moon and Months

The moon has the least effect on earth of all the astronomical phenomena yet described. However, the moon phases–new moon, crescents, half-moon and full moon–were also conspicuous timepieces to many ancient people. Ancient people saw the appearance of a darkened or lightened moon as a regular timepiece for use in dividing up the year. The result is the *kho'-desh* in the Old Testament and the *mane* in the Greek New Testament meaning the month. The movement of the moon around the center of mass of the earth-moon center of gravity is quite complex in the present day orbit of the moon. A discussion of this motion is described in the appendices. The phases of the moon are caused by the shadow of the earth on the moon's face. When the moon is fully darkened by the earth's shadow the moon, sun and earth are said to be in conjunction. In the present, 365¼-day orbit, this does not occur on an even number of days. Nor does it occur at the same time of the year. It will be shown that this was not always the case.

The appearance of the new moon began the Israelites' months and started the day count to the feasts they were to observe throughout the year. A later chapter will show what a confusing exercise this is using the present 365¼-day year. The Bible speaks of a simpler system before our present longer year.

It is the author's opinion that too much has been made of the Jewish "lunar" calendar, which is misleading to the student trying to understand calendar sciences. It is obvious that the self-motion of the earth (rotation), the yearly orbit of the earth around the sun, and the orbit of the moon around the barycenter (center of mass) of the earth-moon are all of equal importance in understanding the calendar and the keeping of the calendar by the ancient Israelites. The reader must consider all of these astronomical events when coming to the Bible to reach an understanding of the biblical time systems.

Time Systems of the Modern Astronomer

We now consider the time systems used by contemporary scientists to measure time. They are important because they are based only on the motion of the heavenly bodies. They form a common reference time system for all other time systems and are used here in the investigation of the miraculous setting of the sun on the dial of Ahaz.

There are four kinds of time systems used in astronomy. The fourth--atomic time--will not be considered because God has not designated anything but celestial motion as the time measuring method for civil timekeeping. The other three are sidereal time, universal time, and ephemeris time. The exact definition of these time systems has been made complex by slight corrections caused by the non-uniform distribution of mass on the earth, etc. If the reader is interested in more details, he is referred to Taff.[3]

The Astronomical Day

The day is the fundamental unit of time keeping by astronomers.

> **Sidereal Time**–This time system is derived from the earth's rotation with respect to the stars. One day is determined by when a particular place on earth (the longitude of Greenwich, England) passes the same position relative to the stars.
> **Universal Time**–This time system is derived from the earth's orbit around the sun. It differs from sidereal time because the earth's orbit around the sun and the apparent passage of the sun past a point on the horizon differs by about four minutes. The result is that the tropical year--the year that is derived from this system--is different than the sidereal year.
> **Ephemeris Time**–This is the time system derived from the use of time as the independent variable in the equations of celestial motion. This time system is absolutely uniform whereas the sidereal and universal time systems are not. This is because of the very small acceleration and deceleration of the earth's rotation and the gradual slowing down of the earth's rotation. Ephemeris time must, therefore, be adjusted to reproduce equivalent time in other time systems.

The Astronomical Year

There are five types of astronomical years.[3]

> **Tropical Year**–The time interval from equinox to equinox (spring or "vernal" equinox to autumnal equinox). The equinox is when the period of light and darkness are equal. However, this definition is insufficient for astronomical purposes. The true equinox takes place when the sun passage along the ecliptic crosses the celestial equator. This was the primary measure of the year used by ancient people. It is, in Ephemeris Time units, 365.2422 days.
> **Sidereal Year**–The time interval for one complete revolution of the Earth around the sun relative to the stars. It is, in Ephemeris Time units, 365.2563 days. Ancient people rarely used this time period (the exception being the Egyptians, who observed the star Sirius' annual motion).
> **Anomalistic Year**–The time interval from perihelion to perihelion. Recall that the perihelion is the shortest distance from the earth to the sun and lies on the axis of the ellipse that tracks the orbit of the earth around the sun throughout the year. It is, in Ephemeris Time units, 365.2596 days.
> **Eclipse Year**–The time interval from lunar node to lunar node. It is, in Ephemeris Time units, 346.6200 days.

The fifth type of year–the Besselian year–will not concern us here. We will not consider any other year apart from the sidereal and tropical years. The sidereal year is used in our astronomical investigations. However, there is no evidence that anything but the tropical year is used in the Bible.

References

1. Quoted in Barnett, J. E.: *Time's Pendulum*. New York: Plenum Publication Corp., 1998.
2. Bullinger, Ethelbert W. *Numbers in Scripture: Its Supernatural Design and Scriptural Significance*. Grand Rapids: Kregel Publications, 1998.
3. Taff, L. G. *Celestial Mechanics: A Computational Guide for the Practitioner*. Hoboken: John Wiley & Sons Inc., 1985.

"When I consider thy heavens, the work of thy fingers, the moon and the stars, which thou hast ordained; What is man, that thou art mindful of him? and the son of man, that thou visitest him?"

(Psalms 8:3-4)

CALENDARS

We have now spent enough time understanding the basis of how ancient people measured time and, particularly, the principles behind how time is measured. The interpretation of these astronomical observations, their groupings, and their association to events leads to the study of chronology and calendars.

Chronology is the science that deals with measuring time by regular divisions and that assigns to events their proper dates.[1] A calendar is a way of grouping days in a manner that allows for regulation of civil life and ecclesiastical observations.[1] In this book, our purpose is to examine the events near the time of Hezekiah, king of Judah and Isaiah the prophet. They lived in the period near the end of the seventh century B. C. Beyond this, chronology is only occasionally referred to. In this chapter, however, we will spend some time examining the history of calendar making and keeping. Once again, the reader is reminded that calendars are the artificial invention of man. The exception is the Divine calendar, discussed at the end of the chapter. Man-made calendars have limitations that must always be validated, first, by God's word and, second, by astronomical principles. An earlier chapter showed that the very basis of time is the connection of an astronomical epoch (instant of time) and an observable event. This is the principle behind Genesis 1:14 and the one in which the author follows absolutely.

Daniel's Image

In the book of Daniel, Chapter 3, the prophet Daniel interprets an incredible vision given to Nebuchadnezzar, king of Babylon. Southgate[2] gives an excellent interpretation of the meaning of this vision. His work will be directly referred to here. Nebuchadnezzar ruled in the early sixth century B. C. and has been accredited with great military and administrative genius. He was a great builder and ruled Babylon as a despot. Included in his territory were countries known today as Iraq, Turkey, Syria, Lebanon, Jordan, Israel, and parts of Egypt and Iran. In the dream, Nebuchadnezzar saw a great metallic statue that towered in the sky. In Daniel 2:39-40, we learn that Nebuchadnezzar was told that the statue contained different metals, each relating to the other in a particular way.

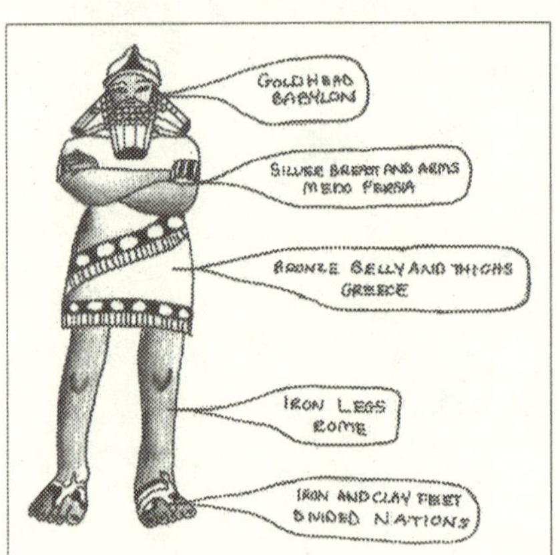

The diagram shows Daniel's image. Daniel's image consists of five parts; a head of gold, silver breasts and arms, bronze belly and thighs, iron legs and iron and clay feet. Daniel's interpretation of this remarkable prophecy was fulfilled to the letter with five great empires.

Daniel 2:39-40	Empire	Approx. Dates
Head of Gold	Babylonian Empire	B. C. 610-540
Breast and Arms of Silver	Persian Empire	B. C. 540-330
Belly and Thighs of Brass	Greek Empire	B. C. 330-190
Legs of Iron	Roman Empire	B. C. 190 – A. D. 475

It will be seen that there is a direct correlation in the development of the modern calendar and Daniel's image, which represents the development of the kingdoms of the world from Daniel's day forward.

The Evolution of the 365¼ Days-in-a-Year Calendar

Our modern calendar from Daniel's day forward can be shown to have its origins in the Babylonian calendar. The Jews changed the name of their months to the Babylonian names when they returned to the land promised to them by God in the fifth century B. C. This can be seen from the table of Jewish months and their references in the Bible.

The Babylonian Legacy– "The Head of Gold"

The Babylonian reckoning of the 365¼-day year would become the foundation for all calendar systems to follow. Many civilizations previous to this, strangely, seemed to have no problem relating days, weeks, months and years. A separation occurred between different peoples after the seventh century B. C. Many, such as the Mayans, Aztecs, Egyptians, the Zoroastrians, etc., had a 360-day year to which they added 5 days or 5¼ days. The obvious question is: *Why did they have a 360-day year in the first place?* It clearly did not fit the astronomical circumstance, as we understand them to be. The Babylonians were the first to create a lunisolar calendar and connect the motion of the moon and the sun into a consistent calendar system. All calendars, thereafter, of the Jews, Medes, Persians, Greeks, Romans and the churches of Christendom have their roots in the Babylonian calendar. They were the "head of gold" in the prophet Daniel's image.

The Babylonian calendar alternated between 29 and 30 days. They reckoned the day from sunset to sunset, just as the Jews. They set the day as 24 hours; 12 hours of daylight and 12 hours of darkness. The hours were of variable lengths of time as the year proceeded from equinox to solstice, back to equinox and solstice again. Nighttime was divided into three equal "watches." Babylonian astronomers learned to divide each day into twelve equal units called beru, and each beru was subdivided into thirty gesh. The Babylonians placed a special significance to lunations in multiples of seven. This is parallel to the Sabbath week introduced in the Bible. The original cycle that related the lunar and solar cycles was called the saros. The saros is a period of 18 years and 11 1/3 days (plus or minus one day depending on a leap year). Later, Babylonian astronomers computed the original lunisolar cycle of 19 years and 235 months with intercalations in years 3, 6, 8, 11, 14, 17 and 19 years in the cycle. Meton & Euctemon and Callippus' lunisolar cycles were based on this original eclipse cycle. The Babylonians divided the year into two seasons: summer and winter. The year began near the spring equinox, the month Nisan. The earlier year was a civil one, beginning in the month Tisri.

Medes and Persians–"Breast and Arms of Silver"

Under the Persian Kings (380 B. C.), the Babylonian astronomers were able to calculate a month of $29^{d}12^{h}44^{m}3.5^{s}$. The Persians standardized the Babylonian calendar across their empire and appear to have made little change in the development of the calendar beyond that prescribed by the Babylonians. Later, the Seleucids and the Parthians maintained the Babylonian calendar.

The Greeks–"Belly and Thighs of Brass"

Once Alexander conquered the Persians, the Persian calendar was adapted to the Babylonian calendar. According to Herodotus, the Greeks learned to use the sundial from the Babylonians.[4] They adopted the Egyptian method of counting twenty-four constant units to create the hour (no doubt influencing the time-reckoning at the time of Christ) but also keeping the earlier method of the Babylonians of keeping a sixty unit divisor of the hour (into what we now call "minutes").[4] In Palestine, the Ptolemies (332–200 B. C.) introduced, briefly, the keeping of the Macedonian calendar. However, there is no evidence that this persisted and the Babylonian calendar eventually was used. In 432 B. C., Meton and Euctemon introduced a 12-year cycle of 12 lunar months and 7 years of 13 lunar months for a total of 235 lunar months. They considered cycles of 29 and 30 day months based on (110 x 29) + (125 x 30) or 6,940 days. The difference is only 5 days in 19 years and yielded an average of 365¼-Day solar year. By comparing their work to the previous work of the Babylonian astronomers, it is clear that their work is based on the earlier Babylonian calendar. Callippus (370–300 B. C.) improved on Meton and Euctemon's cycles. Callippus' cycles consist of four Metonic cycles. He introduced 441 months of 29 days and 499 months of 30 days for a cycle of 27,759 days. By dividing 27,759 ÷ (19 x 4) = 365¼ days exactly. Further improvements were introduced by Hipparchus (150 B. C.) who observed the precession of the equinoxes. This causes a slight change to the time of the vernal equinox, the starting and ending point of the tropical year. The precession causes a migration of the vernal point 2° in 150 years. Both the Assyrians and the Babylonians already knew of the precession of the equinoxes.

The Romans–"Legs of Iron"

The Roman republican calendar was found to cause the seasons to be out of phase with the month and year. In 50 B. C., the vernal equinox appeared in May when it should have appeared in late March: 8 weeks out of phase. The republican calendar had a year of 366¼ days, causing a disparity of one month every 30 years. Julius Caesar invited Sosigenes, an Alexandrian astronomer, to adjust the calendar. Caesar ordered a year of 365 days and an extra day every 4 years (the Julian calendar). Other adjustments were made in 44 B. C., producing a calendar very similar to the present calendar.

The Declining Roman Empire and the Churches of Christendom–"Feet of Iron and Clay"

The Julian year was too long. The true tropical year is approximately 365.242199 days. The Julian calendar was 365.25 days causing the years to be too long resulting in an error of 7 days in 1,000 years. Although this difference is small, by A.D. 1545 the vernal equinox had moved 10 days from its proper date. The primary concern of the Catholic Church was the proper dating of Easter. Roger Bacon, in A.D. 1267, noted the forward progression of the equinox in the year by 1/130 days per year, or, just over 11 minutes per year. However, this error was not corrected for three more centuries.[5] Pope Paul III left the decision to change the calendar to Pope Gregory XIII in A. D. 1572 when the Jesuit astronomer Christopher Clavius was commissioned to change the calendar by papal decree. The vernal equinox was reset back to March 21 by moving the date October 5th forward to become October 15th. Next, the tropical year 365.2422 was adopted, yielding a difference of 3.12 days every 400 years. In what would become the Gregorian calendar--in essence, the calendar we keep today--the day that was supposed to be added every 4th year (the leap year) was omitted at the turn of the century for the "centennial years" (the years 1700, 1800, 1900, etc.) would be added only by centennial years evenly divisible by 400. For example, no leap day would be added for the years 1700, 1800, 1900 but a day would be added in the year 2000. These adjustments were by no means adopted uniformly throughout Asia and Europe. Some countries rejected its implementation until the eighteenth century. For example, France kept a republican calendar until January 1, 1806 when the Gregorian calendar was finally adopted. The Germans preferred to keep a calendar based on the observations of the astronomer Tycho Brahe.

Important to our investigation was the decision made by the western Roman Catholic Church to ensure that Easter, the church festival of the death and resurrection of Jesus Christ, fell on a Sunday near the vernal equinox. We say "church festival" because nowhere in the New Testament is it commanded that a particular day of the year be celebrated. The Passover occurred on the 14 Nisan in the Jewish year. The month Nisan occurs at the same time of the year as March/April in the modern calendar. Setting the Sunday after the appearance of the Full Moon on or after the vernal equinox was the manner of dating Easter. The reader will recall that in the Old Testament, in the time previous to the seventh century, the date of the New Moon was always Abib (later named Nisan). A count of 14 days would signal the occurrence of the Passover. We know that Jesus was crucified during the celebration of the Passover. The church further decreed that if the Passover fell on a Sunday, Easter would be held 7 days later. To accomplish this they assigned letters to mark each day. January 1 was assigned the letter 'A,' January 2 'B' and so on. Once the first Sunday is determined to be a certain letter, all dates having this letter are possible candidates. The candidate Sunday occurs between March 25 and April 25. Against each date the number 1 through 19 was placed, indicating which of the 19 years would yield a Full Moon on that day. These were referred to as "golden numbers." This was introduced in A. D. 530. A new cycle was created, which, when working backward, began with a New Moon on A.D. January 1, 1. This is how our A. D. years began. The general belief was that this was the birth of Jesus but such an assertion is unsubstantiated by the Bible. Each year is given a golden number by dividing the year by 19 and adding a remainder of 1. A remainder of zero gives a golden number of 19. Later, this method was abandoned when it was determined that the astronomical Full Moon could differ by as much as two days from the observed Full Moon. A system called the epact was introduced to give a more accurate result, based on the use of a calendar that had alternating days of 29 and 30 just as the Babylonians had used. The epact system was based on Metonic cycles and had to have the same solar corrections attached to it as were made in the Gregorian calendar.

It is apparent that reasonable attempts were made to ensure that the astronomical significance of the Passover/Easter celebration has been preserved. The slow adoption of the new calendar style of the Gregorian calendar and the calculation of Easter were sometimes rejected for astronomical reasons. For example, the German and Swedish Protestants rejected the Catholic determination of Easter, preferring to use astronomical tables of the astronomer Tycho Brahe.

Planet	Babylonian Name	Roman Name	Anglo-Saxon Name	English Name
Sun	Shanah	Sol	Sun	Sunday
Moon	Sin	Luna	Moon	Monday
Mars	Nergal	Mars	Tiew	Tuesday
Mercury	Nabu	Mercurius	Woden	Wednesday
Jupiter	Marduk	Jupiter	Thor	Thursday
Venus	Ishtar	Venus	Freya	Friday
Saturn	Ninurta	Saturnus	Saturn	Saturday

Genealogy of the Days of the Week Showing its Babylonian Origins[6]

The B. C. and A. D. Years

We have seen that the division of the calendar into B. C. and A. D. years does not have a biblical basis, and so, based on the principles set out for our investigation, it is to be viewed with some skepticism. B. C. stands for "before Christ." The end of B. C. year 1 is supposed to mark the birth year of Jesus Christ. A. D. "anno Domini" year 1 immediately begins from this date. The problem is that the birth year of Jesus as determined by early calendar creators was uncertain.

Another time system commonly attempted is called A. M. *anno Mundi* or the *age of the world*. This presumes that it is possible to date all events from the Adamic creation forward. It was originally of Jewish origin and was developed through examination of the chronology of the Bible. This also is a matter of great dispute and is anything but resolved. In *Chronikon Hebraikon*[3], J. Thomas lists several attempts to determine the B. C. year of the Creation:

Source	B. C. Year Of Creation
The Septuagint Computation	5586
Samaritan Text	4305
Hebrew Text, as interpreted by chronologists	4161
English Bible	4004
Josephus, according to Playfair	5555
Josephus, according to Jackson	5481
Josephus, according to Hales	5402
Josephus, according to Universal History	4698
Chinese Jews	4079
Jewish Computation	3760
Clemens Alexandrinus	4624
Hales	5411
Origen, A. D. 230	4830
Shimeall	4132
Usher	4004
Luther	3961

It is clear that basing a time system on A. M. years is also potentially confusing. The principal difficulty is creating a comprehensive--and widely accepted--chronology of all of biblical events. Most generally accept Usher's date of 4004 B. C. as the most biblically sound date for creation. However, to this day, the full chronology of the Bible is still very much in dispute. Recent attempts by Jones[4] based on modern discoveries are probably more accurate.

The Julian Day Cycle

This book uses the astronomical approach and then converts these values into calendar dates based on the best modern calculations available for converting these astronomical dates. For our purposes, our base time scale is the astronomical time scale that is measured in ephemeris years. The diagram shows the connection between astronomical years and B. C. and A. D. years.

1 B. C.	1 A. D.	
-1	0	+1

B.C. and A.D. Years versus Astronomical Years Showing the Missing 0th Year

A Julian period is a cycle made up of 7,980 years. It is further made up of a Metonic cycle of 19 years, a solar cycle of 28 years and an indiction cycle of 15 years. The solar cycle represents the 28-year cycle of 52 weeks of 7 days repeated every 4 years (due to the day added in a leap year). The solar cycle is the 28-year period when the day of the week repeats. For example, Jan. 17, 1999 is a Sunday. It will repeat as a Sunday on Jan. 17, 2027. The indiction year cycle was a fiscal cycle and is not an astronomical cycle. So 19 x 28 x 15 = 7,980 years. Scaliger traced these three cycles back to January 1, 4713 B. C. The Julian period has no use in the modern calendar but is the foundation of the Julian day used in astronomy. It is used because it is the only calendar cycle where the days are free from combinations of weeks and months. Astronomers use this cycle and take noon as the instant of time zero. Therefore, the Julian Day cycle origin is the fundamental epoch of the Universal Time (U. T.) system used in modern astronomy. The conversion between them is 12^h, Jan. 1, 4713 B. C. = 0 JD.[Y]

It can be seen that calendars group days in various ways. Many of the calendars have been seen to be flawed and were created to suit a belief prevalent at the time. This is insufficient for our purposes. Modern methods in celestial mechanics and astronomy provide the means of ensuring a far more rigorous timekeeping methodology. Rules are then employed which consistently convert this time system--the ephemeris time system--to various calendars.

The Old Testament Calendar

The Old Testament relates the observance of feasts to certain days of certain months. The beginning of months is set by the appearance of the New Moon, one of the lunar phases. The feasts were to be kept at certain seasons of the year.

Sacred Month	*Civil Month*	*Pre-Exilic Name*	*Post-Exilic Name*	*Reference*	*Modern Equivalent*	*Season*	*Feast*
1	7	Abib	Nisan	Ex. 7:2,Ne. 2:1	March-April	Spring Latter Rains Barley harvest Flax harvest	14: Passover (Ex. 12:18) 15-21: Unleavened Bread (Lev. 23:6)
2	8	Ziw	Iyyar	I Ki. 7:1,37	April-May	Dry Season	14: Later Passover (Nu. 9:10,11)
3	9		Siwan	Est. 8:9	May-June	Early figs	6: Pentecost (Lev. 23) Feast of Weeks
4	10		Tammuz	Eze. 8:14	June-July	Grape harvest	
5	11		Ab		July-August	Olive harvest	
6	12		Elul	Ne. 6:15	August-September	Dates and summer figs	
7	1	Ethanim	Tisri	I Ki. 8:2	September-October	Early rains	1: Trumpets (Nu. 29:1) 10: Day of Atonement (Lev. 16:29) 15-21: Tabernacles (Lev. 23:34) 22: Solemn Assembly (Lev. 23:36)
8	2	Bul	Marheswan	1 Ki. 6:38	October-November	Ploughing Winter figs	
9	3		Kislew	Ne. 1:1	November-December	Sowing	
10	4		Tebet	Est. 2:16	December-January	Rains	
11	5		Sebat	Zech. 1:7	January-February	Almond blossom	
12	6		Adar	Ezr. 6:15	February-March	Citrus fruit blossom	

Table of the Months of the Biblical Year (after Bruce[1])

The table shows the occurrence of the months, their equivalence in our modern calendar, and the observances set by God for the Israelites to follow.[5] For example, the feast of ingathering must be celebrated in the autumn after harvest. In the 365¼-day year, there are not an evenly divisible number of months in a solar year. It is necessary, then, to create methods for transforming the grouping of days of the month into the groupings of days of the year. These transformations are called lunisolar transformations. Throughout the ages, several kinds have been employed and their history will be discussed below. However, the Bible never refers to the use of any lunisolar transformation employed by chronologists of the 365¼-day calendar. The New Testament never even mentions a calendar. The insertion of days, weeks or months–called intercalation–is never mentioned and is unscriptural. The Bible refers only to a 30-day month, a 12-month year and a 360-day year. The Bible refers to a specific day of the month as the end of the year (Exodus 23:16) even though it was not possible to achieve this in the Jewish calendar without intercalating a certain number of days.

The accompanying diagram shows the naming of months and seasons in the Scriptures. The Scriptures teach, that,

1. The 15th day of their original first month--the month of Ethanim--was the end of the year and hence their New Year's Day. This is at the time of September/October in our present calendar. This was marked by the feast of ingathering (alternately, the feast of tabernacles). *"And the feast of harvest, the firstfruits of thy labours, which thou hast sown in the field: and the feast of ingathering, which is in the end of the year, when thou hast gathered in thy labours out of the field."* (Exodus 23:16).
2. Their "new" beginning of the year became their new first month after their exodus from Egypt. This is the month Abib. Abib is presently March/April. Ethanim then became their 7th month. The day after the Passover was recognized on the 15th day of the month of Abib. *"And they departed from Rameses in the first month, on the fifteenth day of the first month; on the morrow after the passover the children of Israel went out with an high hand in the sight of all the Egyptians."* (Numbers 33:3).
3. The month began with the appearance of the new moon.
4. After the exile, the names of the months changed to Babylonian names. For example, the month Abib became the month Nisan and the month Ethanim became the month Tisri.
5. The day was marked from sunset to sunset or from *"even (`ereb) unto even"* (Leviticus 23:32). It was originally divided into three parts (Psalms 55:17). *"The heat of the day"* (1 Sam. 11:11) was at our nine o'clock, and *"the cool of the day"* just before sunset (Genesis 3:8). Before the exile, the Jews divided the night into three watches, (1) from sunset to midnight (Lam. 2:19); (2) from midnight till the cock-crowing (Judges 7:19); and (3) from the cock-crowing till sunrise (Exodus 14:24).
6. The Bible recognizes non-astronomical time periods such as a week (7 consecutive days), sabbath years (7 consecutive years), and jubilee years (7 × 7 = 49 year cycles). Detailed description of these biblical time systems occurs in a later chapter.

Many of the common practices kept by the Jews to accommodate our present 365¼-day year are never discussed in the Scriptures. For example, the Bible never talks of intercalation of days or months, as is the current practice, in order to keep the moon and the sun cycles in sync. Yet, it is clearly necessary lest the seasons gradually "wander" through the calendar over the years. It is peculiar that this is the case. In fact, previous to the time of Hezekiah, the evidence points to a more uniform calendar consisting of 30-day months with 12 months making up a 360-day year. Additional evidence for this proposition is the subject of later chapters.

The New Testament Calendar

In the New Testament, the Jews followed the calendars of the Romans and used the calendar principles that were common to them at that time. This, as we have seen, originated from the Babylonians (during the Jewish exile in Babylon) and subsequently was handed down to the Medes and Persians, the Greeks, and finally the Romans. It is interesting that Daniel is the first to use the principle of the hour as a period of sunlight during the day. The division of the day into twelve hours is a departure from the original Hebrew practice of recognizing the day as sunset to sunset and dividing the night and day into three watches each. The New Testament times recognized a day began at sunrise and finished at sunset with twelve hours of variable length during the day: *"Jesus answered, Are there not twelve hours in the day?"* (John 11:9). The night divisions followed the Roman practice of divisions into four watches. This differed slightly from the Greek method of dividing the night into three watches.

In the ancient world, all the nations around Canaan recognized the equinox as the true beginning of the year. It was easily recognized by the fact the light and dark were of equal length. Also, the Sun would rise precisely in the east on this day and set precisely in the west. It is not coincidental that the end of the year (the month Ethanim) would contain the autumnal equinox and the month Abib contains the spring or vernal equinox. This would make the day after Passover and the feast of ingathering both occur on the equinox. However, the Scriptures never say that the equinox was the beginning of the year; it is implied by strong evidence.

References

1. Bruce, F. F. *The New Bible Dictionary*. J. D. Douglas, Ed., Grand Rapids: Wm. B. Eerdmans Publishing Co., 1962.
2. Southgate, P. J. *Thine is the Kingdom*. Birmingham: Dawn Book Supply, 1986.
3. Thomas, J. *Chronikon Hebraikon*. Birmingham: Christadelphian, 1949.
4. Jones, F. N. *Chronology of the Old Testament: A Return to Basics,* 15th Ed., The Woodlands: Master Books, Inc., 2004.
5. Bickerman, E. J. *Chronology of the Ancient World*, Ithaca: Cornell University Press, 1982.

"Seek him that maketh the seven stars and Orion, and turneth the shadow of death into the morning, and maketh the day dark with night: that calleth for the waters of the sea, and poureth them out upon the face of the earth: The LORD is his name:"

(Amos 5:8)

3

ORBITAL MOTION AND GOD'S POWER OVER THE NATURAL WORLD

Having now come to an understanding of how time is interpreted, we must turn to the more fundamental principles of astronomy and celestial mechanics to begin investigating the physical principles behind the keeping of time. This will be necessary for understanding later evidence of how the miracle occurred during the time of Hezekiah.

The reader should now be aware that we are entering a mathematical portion of our journey of understanding. Understanding some of these difficult concepts can best be achieved with the guide of someone trained in these areas.

The Orbital Laws of Kepler

It was Copernicus who is widely credited with the discovery that the earth orbits around the sun. Johannes Kepler used the astronomer Tyco Brahe's calculations to establish the three laws that govern the orbit of the earth around the sun. He published the first two in A. D. 1609 and a third law in 1632[1-2]. The three laws are as follows:

1. The orbit of the planets around the sun occurs along an oval curve called an ellipse. The definition of the ellipse is that the sum of the distance from the ellipse foci to the orbital position of the planet is a constant. The Sun is at one of these foci.
2. The radius vector of a planet, with its origin at the sun, sweeps out equal areas at equal times.
3. The square of the orbital period is proportional to the cube of the mean distance to the sun.

The Orbital Laws of Newton

Isaac Newton's work *Principia*,[3] published in A. D. 1695 set out the laws of gravitation from which the modern scientific field of celestial mechanics is founded. His work was based on Kepler's calculations. Newton's laws allow precise calculations of orbital motion. Newton's laws of motion are as follows:

1. Every body continues in a state of rest, or of uniform motion in a straight line, unless compelled by an impressed force to change that state.
2. The rate of change of momentum is proportional to the impressed force, and takes place in the direction in which the forces act.
3. To every action corresponds an equal and opposite reaction.

Modern space travel has substantiated these laws to a very high degree. Software programs--including those used to develop the findings of this book--that calculate the position of the moon, a satellite orbiting earth, a comet orbiting the sun and a space vehicle exploring the outer planets of the solar system are all based on the work of Kepler and Newton. Modern calculations requiring high precision use the mathematical equations that resulted from these laws. For example, lasers are used to determine locations on the moon with no less accuracy than ±10 centimeters.[2] And yet, comparable results can be achieved using the laws of Kepler and Newton.

The Orbit of Mercury–The Exception to the Laws of Kepler and Newton

An important exception to the laws of Newton and Kepler occurs in the planetary motion of Mercury in our solar system. Mercury's point of perihelion precesses forward.[4] You will recall that the perihelion is the point of the orbit when the planet is closest to the sun. All of the other planets return almost precisely to the point in space where they originated exactly one year previously, except for Mercury. Mercury, whose orbit is closest to the sun, has a perihelion that advances forward by forty-three seconds of arc per century. Over a period of over three million years, this causes the perihelion to traverse the entire orbit. Einstein's theory of relativity explains this anomaly to be due to the curvature of space-time in his general theory of relativity. General relativity is a subject that will not be addressed in this book and our focus will be on the earth-moon orbits that *can be* entirely described by Kepler's and Newton's laws.

Application of the Laws of Kepler and Newton to the Study of Bible Time Systems

We do not deviate in any way from the principles of Scripture through the use of these laws. Genesis 1:14 gives man the right to use the heavenly bodies as time measuring instruments. Kepler and Newton's work describes (using mathematical equations) *how they work.* For example if you purchased a mechanical pocket watch, and you took the watch home, removed the screws fastening the face to its backing, then, by carefully observing how the gears and springs worked, you would be able to determine how the watch worked. The accuracy and precision of your analysis could easily be verified by comparing your results with what can be plainly read on the clock face. God is the creator of the universe and has set in motion the heavenly bodies that we use to tell time. Men have been able to devise methods whereby they can measure what the Lord has created, nothing more.

Orbital Motion of the Earth around the Sun

The first section describes the mathematical formulae used as the foundation for the calculation of the orbital motion of the earth. For those who are not mathematically oriented, this section can be skipped. These formulae are used in later chapters to compute the effect of changing the sun's position relative to the earth's during the time of Hezekiah, king of Judah.

The next section describes the orbital elements. Their primary usefulness is as a glossary of terms referred to in other chapters.

Mathematical Formulae for the Earth's Orbit around the Sun

Kepler's second law has an interesting and important consequence,

$$h = rv_{\perp}$$

Where h is the orbital angular momentum, r is the distance separating the orbiting mass and the orbited mass (the earth-moon center of mass and the sun, respectively) and $v_\perp$ is the component of the velocity of the orbiting mass at right angles (tangential) to the direction of the separation distance r. The quantity h is constant for two masses, as in the sun and earth-moon problem. This is an important factor for validating whether our orbital calculations are correct. A 360-day orbit and a 365¼-day orbit will have a single but different value of h for its entire orbit.

Kepler's third law mathematically states,

$$P^2 = \frac{4\pi^2}{\mu} a^3$$

Where P is the orbital period, a is the length of the semi-major axis of the orbit and μ is,

$$\mu = k^2 (m_A + m_B)$$

Where A and B refer to the two orbiting bodies A and B. In our case, it is the sun and the combined mass of the earth and moon at their center of mass. The importance of this relation is that it allows the calculation of the period (for example, for a 360-day year or a 365¼-day year) from some of the orbital elements. This is also found to be very useful in the search for a plausible explanation for the sun going down on Ahaz's dial, discussed in a later chapter.

Newton's law of gravitation states that all mass in the universe attracts every other mass with equal and opposite force in proportion to the mass values and inversely proportional to the square of the distance. The force due to gravitation between two bodies (A and B) can be determined. Using the nomenclature of Brouwer and Clemence.[5]

$$F = \frac{k^2 m_A m_B}{r^2}$$

Where F is the force, m is the mass of the body, r is the separation distance between the two bodies and k is the universal gravitational constant.

The orbital motion of the earth around the sun is assumed to occur on a plane called the *ecliptic*. This allows us to look only at the two-dimensional aspects of this problem. Further, we assume that the two bodies that are moving under mutual gravitation are the sun and the center of mass of the earth and moon. The justification for this approach is shown in the appendix.

This reduces the problem to solving the differential equations,

$$\frac{dv_x}{dt} = \frac{d^2x}{dt^2}, \quad \frac{dv_y}{dt} = \frac{d^2y}{dt^2}$$

where (x, y) are the x and y coordinates in a Cartesian coordinate system, t is the time, r is the separation distance.

The sun's mass is very large relative to the mass of the earth and moon. We can determine the location of the earth at any time by noting that,

$$v_x = \frac{dx}{dt}, \quad v_y = \frac{dy}{dt}$$

Where v is the velocity, and that,

$$\frac{d^2x}{dt^2} = -\mu\frac{x}{r^3}, \quad \frac{d^2y}{dt^2} = -\mu\frac{y}{r^3}$$

where,

$$x = x(t), \quad y = y(t)$$

These equations are not directly solvable when multiple masses are considered and must be determined using a mathematical procedure called *numerical integration*. While these calculations can be done with pen and paper, to do so is extremely laborious. The computations can simply be transformed into algorithms. A computer program was written to solve the problem of the earth-moon center of mass orbiting the sun using a numerical integration method referred to as *the 4th order Runge-Kutta method*. The procedures used and the restrictions on its application are discussed in the appendices.

When there are only two masses considered the problem can be solved directly. This type of solution is called an *analytical solution*. This approach is useful because it yields exact solutions and serves as a comparison to the results computed using numerical integration. This method requires a separate derivation and is also outlined in the appendices.

The Role of the Miraculous

It is now necessary to place restrictions on the preceding discussion. We must put its teaching in its proper place. We repeat an earlier precept: the works of men are merely models of the actual movements of the heavenly bodies created and maintained by God. Scientific principles do not and cannot account for the miraculous. Biologists cannot allow for a resurrection from the dead, chemists cannot fathom water turning into wine, nor would many physicists accept the miraculous displacement of the sun from its ancient position in space to a new position. Denial of the miraculous power of God is to deny His power over our physical world and His very existence. It is currently fashionable to refer to God's power as a kind of benign force without purpose except for the presumed benefit of man. Biblical evidence shows otherwise. God performs miracles to further *His* purposes and never to suit the purposes of man solely. We will show that, in the time of Hezekiah, God moved the sun and transformed what was a 360-day orbit with twelve 30-day months to our present 365¼-day year. We will use scientific models to establish the *effect* of God's intervention but not the *cause*. We do not have to have a proof of a cause when we believe in the miraculous. However, we cannot allow "the miraculous" to provide license to do as we please with the laws of nature. There is abundant proof that God does not act in this manner.

Governing Principle of the Miraculous

God claims that He can and will intervene in man's affairs. He has also stated that He will use His omnipotence to overrule the laws of nature when He chooses. The mainstream philosophers of modern times too often become overly mechanistic in their interpretation of life. There is no longer any place or time for the spiritual because it cannot be proved to their satisfaction. In opposition, the Scriptures teach that God's unseen spiritual power pervades all things:

"Through faith we understand that the worlds were framed by the word of God, so that things which are seen were not made of things which do appear." (Heb. 11:3; see also 2 Corinthians 4:18)

We cannot look to the things which are seen for our ultimate guidance but rather look to God who has framed all things with His word. The prophet Daniel says, ***"And he changeth the times and the seasons: he removeth kings, and setteth up kings: he giveth wisdom unto the wise, and knowledge to them that know understanding"*** (Daniel 2:21). Since the latter part of this verse is literal, what about the first part? Has God literally changed the times and the seasons? The answer is yes and it will be established in a later chapter. All speak of His Divine power and intervention in man's affairs through these powers beyond our ability to understand.

A scientific work that allows for God's power to overrule well-established physical laws is certain to be criticized and dismissed by many. Nevertheless, the man of God understands that the wisdom of God appears as foolishness to the natural man and that the foolishness of God is greater than the greatest wisdom that man can conceive (cf. 1 Corinthians 1:25).

A Divine Cause

A mechanistic *cause and effect* approach to understanding the miraculous is fraught with deficiency. At first this approach might seem to be on firm ground. The hailstones that killed Joshua's enemies at Gibeon (Josh. 10:11) could be attributed to a fortuitous nearby passage of a comet. The star that guided the wise men of the east to Jesus' birthplace might also be presumed to be a natural astronomical phenomenon. The mechanist is happy so far because he has yet to put himself *on the spot* to explain the unexplainable. However, he quickly runs into problems. He struggles to explain how *a strong east wind* could part the Red Sea in order that Moses and the children of Israel might pass through. He finds it impossible to explain how Jesus turned water into wine (John 2:1-11). Not only was it wine but it was fine, aged wine! The mechanist cannot explain this miracle using any known natural laws so he substitutes "workable theories" where he sees fit. For example, he might say that Jesus created the illusion that it was wine by some kind of paranormal influence. This can only be admitted if we deny the plain truth of the verse and so we are no longer the instructed but we become the instructor: ***"But the natural man receiveth not the things of the Spirit of God: for they are foolishness unto him: neither can he know them, because they are spiritually discerned"*** (1 Corinthians 2:14). Perhaps he might even say that Jesus altered the sensory perception of the bodies of the drinkers. It quickly becomes foolish when we will not attribute a Divine cause to the miraculous. The Divine cause willed that water would become wine and the laws of physics are either altered or overruled; which, we cannot say. Whatever power the holy spirit has over our physical world, the water in the jugs became fine, aged wine with all of its physical attributes.

A Natural Effect

An equally unfortunate mistake is to take the Divine cause too far and attribute a Divine effect. For example, many have considered the miraculous long day of Joshua: ***"Then spake Joshua to the LORD in the day when the LORD delivered up the Amorites before the children of Israel, and he said in the sight of Israel, Sun, stand thou still upon Gibeon; and thou, Moon, in the valley of Ajalon. And the sun stood still, and the moon stayed, until the people had avenged themselves upon their enemies. Is not this written in the book of Jasher? So the sun stood still in the midst of heaven, and hasted not to go down about a whole day"*** (Josh. 10:12,13). The obvious explanation is that God stopped the rotation of the earth and achieved the described effect. A physicist[6] wrote a rebuttal of this explanation in which he described the net effect of suddenly stopping the earth. He mentioned tectonic effects (ex. earthquakes, etc.) but most importantly, he showed that the earth's surface would heat up to the boiling point destroying all human life.[1f] In our zeal to defend a Biblical statement, we might mistakenly attribute Divine intervention to the physical effect. Such a proposition has no support in the Scriptures. Water changes into wine and has all of the physical and chemical attributes of the same. The physical effect of taste, texture, composition, etc. are all those of wine. The collapsing walls of water worked their natural effect on Pharaoh's army as Moses and the children of Israel passed safely to the other side. They were no doubt crushed by the force of the water and subsequently drowned. We call this principle *Divine Cause, Natural Effect.* An investigation of the Scriptures will show it to be the rule.

This principle will be used in later chapters when the miracle achieved during the time of Hezekiah is described in detail. It allows us to use the physical and mathematical models of celestial mechanics to model the effect of God's intervention in the "times and seasons" of mankind. However, no physical explanation can be made for Divine cause. It will simply be accepted as fact and truth.

References

1. Halliday, D., Resnick, R. Walker, J. *Fundamentals of Physics*. Vol. 2, 4th Ed., New York: John Wiley & Sons, 1974.
2. Taff, L. G. *Celestial Mechanics: A Computational Guide for the Practitioner*. Hoboken: Wiley Interscience, 1985.
3. Newton, Isaac. *Principia, Volume 1, The Motion of Bodies*. Berkley: University of California, 1974.
4. Rindler, W. *Essential Relativity*. 2nd Ed., Springer-Verlag. New York, 1977.
5. Brouwer, D., Clemence, G. M. *Methods of Celestial Mechanics*. New York & London: Academic Press, 1961.
6. Sagan, C. "An Analysis of Worlds in Collision," in *Scientists Confront Velikovsky*. Donald Goldsmith, Ed. Ithaca: Cornell University Press, 1977.

---

1 [f] Estimated average temperature increase for the Earth is $\Delta T \approx 100° K$. The near surface temperature increase would be $\Delta T \approx 240° K$, killing most life.

"In the six hundredth year of Noah's life, in the second month, the seventeenth day of the month, the same day were all the fountains of the great deep broken up, and the windows of heaven were opened. ... And the waters returned from off the earth continually: and after the end of the hundred and fifty days the waters were abated. And the ark rested in the seventh month, on the seventeenth day of the month, upon the mountains of Ararat." (Genesis 7:11, 8:3-4)

THE EVIDENCE FOR A 360 DAY YEAR

Biblical Evidence

The Old Testament clearly points to an ancient year comprised of 360 days made up of 12 months of 30 days exactly. The Scriptures speak of a simplicity and harmony between the times measured from sun and moon observations. And yet the subject has been made so difficult due to the now-observed complexity and discord between time systems created by sun and moon observation. The moon does not have a synodic period of 30 days; it is about 29½ days. We observe today a 365¼-day year and cannot reconcile the differences between it and what Divine Scripture teaches us. We have become so accustomed to ancient chronologists and Bible scholars describing the principles behind inserting days, hours, minutes and seconds to harmonize the sun and moon times with various calendars that we might stop questioning the wonderful simplicity of their descriptions. Some even attempt to explain the discordance with Bible fact is due to an apparent disinterest of the deity in absolute precision. Isaac Newton recognized the fact that all nations previously had a literal 360-day year[21]: "*All nations, before the just length of the solar year was known, reckoned months by the course of the moon, and years by the return of winter and summer, spring and autumn; and in making calendars for their festivals, they reckoned thirty days to a lunar month, and twelve lunar months to a years, taking the nearest round numbers, whence came the division of the ecliptic into 360 degrees.*"

In this section, we will examine the Scriptural evidence for a simple, 360-day year. In a later section we will review the work of other chronologists whose studies of ancient astronomers clearly shows evidence for a 360-day year as well.

The Old Testament Account of the Flood

The flood account is the first reference in Scripture to the relations between the daily, monthly and yearly time systems. It provides the most compelling biblical evidence for a 360-day year. In the six hundredth year of Noah's life, the flood began: ***"In the six hundredth year of Noah's life, in the second month, the seventeenth day of the month, the same day were all the fountains of the great deep broken up, and the windows of heaven were opened"*** (Genesis 7:11). This verse, for the first time, relates the sun, moon and earth as time measuring instruments. The month is governed by the appearance of the New Moon and completes its cycle when a subsequent New Moon is observed. We are told that it was the "*second month,*" which relates to a point in the yearly solar cycle. This is the first scriptural reference to the lunisolar cycle. We are told that it was "*the seventeenth day of the month,*" meaning the earth completed seventeen rotations on its own axis from the observance of the New Moon to that day inclusive.

We then learn: ***"And the waters prevailed upon the earth an hundred and fifty days ... And the waters returned from off the earth continually: and after the end of the hundred and fifty days the waters were abated. And the ark rested in the seventh month, on the seventeenth day of the month, upon the mountains of Ararat"***(Genesis 7:24, Genesis 8:3-4).

The text is unambiguous when taken directly. There are 150 days between the 17th day of the second month and the 17th day of the seventh month meaning there are 5 months of 30 days each. No other interpretation is possible. Nevertheless, faced with the admission that the ancient celestial motions were different from today's (and with no "scientific" theories to rely on), various interpretations are necessarily proffered.

One alternate explanation is that the account omits the intercalated days. The problem with this interpretation is that it is tantamount to saying that the word of God cannot be counted on for stating simple fact. If we take the actual time from New Moon to New Moon we have 29½ days x 5 = 147½ days, 2½ days short of what the Bible says. By not allowing that there are 30 days in the month we must also reject the divinely appointed method of measuring the month. Another explanation is established by taking the period of Genesis 7:11 to Genesis 8:14 as 12 synodical months yielding 354 days. In Genesis 8:14 it says, ***"And in the second month, on the seven and twentieth day of the month, was the earth dried."*** The additional 11 days are taken as representing the 11 additional days that make up the (present) solar year of 365 days. To accept this explanation we would have to allow a year of 354 days when it is nowhere else described in the Bible. Worst, it does not explain the 150-day period described in Genesis 8. In absence of an explanation which does not deny the plain truth of the biblical text, the most reasonable is offered by Velikovsky[1]: *"... these lunar months were thirty days long, with no months of twenty-nine days in between, and as the year was composed of twelve such months, with no additional days or intercalated months, the Bible exegetes could find no way of reconciling the three figures: 354 days, or twelve lunar months of twenty-nine and half days each; 360 days, or a multiplex of twelve times thirty; and 365¼ days, the present length of the year."* In other words, no reasonable explanation can be offered for the 150-day period except for accepting that the orbital motions at the time of Noah were different than they are now. We propose that, during the days of Noah, there was an actual 360-day year made up of 12 months of 30 days each. We leave the description of why we no longer have this 360-day year to a later chapter.

Prior to the flood, time is measured as an accumulation of yearly births at a point in time of the life of the father: ***"And Adam lived an hundred and thirty years, and begat a son in his own likeness, after his image; and called his name Seth"*** (Genesis 5:3). From this we learn that Seth was born in the 131st year of Adam's life. As previously explained, we take a year as the completion of a sun's cycle for this is what the Hebrew word for year means. We have also learned that one complete cycle is when the sun returns to exactly the same spot in the sky. We could say, "*Seth was born at the completion of 131 complete cycles of the sun's apparent motion in the sky since Adam's birth.*" Later we learn, ***"And Seth lived an hundred and five years, and begat Enos"*** (Genesis 5:6). This information allows us to create a biblical chronology.

Other Biblical References

In Deuteronomy 34:8, Deuteronomy 21:13 and Numbers 20:29, reference is made to the period of mourning as being one month of 30 days. In King David's time (about 1000 B. C.), 12 overseers were to look after the affairs of Israel: ***"Now the children of Israel after their number, to wit, the chief fathers and captains of thousands and hundreds, and their officers that served the king in any matter of the courses, which came in and went out month by month throughout all the months of the year, ..."*** (2 Chronicles 27:1). Verses 2-15 of 2 Chronicles 27 list the names of all twelve overseers. Note how it says "*all the months of the year.*" No mention is made of an intercalated month. Similarly, King Solomon had twelve officers: ***"And Solomon had twelve officers over all Israel, which provided victuals for the king and his household: each man his month in a year made provision"*** (1 Kings 4:7).

Historical Evidence

We have shown that Scripture does indeed support the idea that the ancient year was 360 days long. It is reasonable to expect that the historical records of other ancient civilizations would also reveal this simple fact. It will be found that this is true. We quote extensively the work of Velikovsky[1] who, in turn, quotes numerous other scholarly workers, who also show overwhelming evidence for a 360-day year. Some aspects of Velikovsky's work are demonstrably flawed but his citations are useful for our present purpose. He summarizes the evidence for a 360-day year convincingly in Chapter 8 of his book.

As you read the evidence, note that the conclusions are based on astronomical observations. It is so obviously impossible that all of these civilizations made the wrong observations in exactly the same way. These historical records show that there was an actual 360-day year.

Ancient India

In India, texts of the Veda period relate a 360-day year. "*All Veda texts speak uniformly and exclusively of a year of 360 days. Passages in which this length of year is directly stated are found in all the Brahmanas.*"[2] Further: "*It is striking that the Vedas nowhere mention an intercalary period, and while repeatedly stating that the year consists of 360 days, nowhere refer to the five or six days that actually are part of the solar year.*" Thibaut[2] further states that the Hindu year consisted of 360 days, 12 months each of 30 days (just as Scripture says it was). The Brahmanic literature has the moon crescent for 15 days and waning for 15 days. They also say that the sun moved north for 180 days and then south for 180 days.[2] Note that these are astronomical observations; why would they record wrong positions for the sun and moon? Thibaut[2] apparently cannot explain his own findings despite the acknowledged sophistication of the astronomical methods employed by the ancient Indians: "*That these are not conventional inexact data, but definitely wrong notions, is shown by the passage in Nidana-Sutra, which says that the Sun remain 13½ days in each of the 27 Naksatras, and thus the solar year is calculated as 360 days long.*" And, "*Fifteen days are assigned to each half-Moon period; that this is too much is nowhere admitted.*"[2] In the Varaha Mihira, the synodical periods of the planets are recorded. These, states Velikovsky, are easy to determine against the background of the stars. However, they are 5 days too short for Saturn, 5 days too short for Jupiter, 11 days too short for Mars, 8-9 days too short for Venus, and less than 2 days too short for Mercury. Velikovsky records that, "*In a solar system in which the Earth revolves around the Sun in 360 days, the synodical periods of Jupiter and Saturn would be about 5 days shorter than they are at present, and that of Mercury less than 2 days shorter.*" Thibaut states that, "*What is extraordinary are the durations assigned to the synodical revolutions ... To meet in Hindu astronomy with a set of numerical quantities widely differing from those generally accepted is indeed so startling that one at first feels strongly inclined to doubt of the soundness of the text ... Moreover, each figure is given twice over.*" In a later period, the Hindu calendar was reformed to a 365¼-day year. Velikovsky records that this calendar reformation occurred in the seventh century B.C.

Ancient Persia

In Persia, the ancient year was 360 days with 12 months of 30 days. Only in the seventh century B. C. were 5 *Gatha* days added to the calendar[3]. The *Bundahis* was a sacred book of the ancient Persians. It records 180 days from winter solstice to summer solstice. Note again that these astronomical observations would clearly not represent the facts were they applied to a 365¼-day year. Could both the ancient Indians and Persians possibly record the same error? The 5 *Gatha* days are a later addition to a 360-day year cycle.

Ancient Babylon

In ancient Babylon, a 360-day year was observed[4]. Their year consisted of twelve months of thirty days with each month computed from the appearance of the New Moon. Duncan[5] records of the predecessors of the Babylonians, the Sumerians: "*Sumerians by the twenty-first century B. C. had developed a ... system founded on a calendar year of 360 days. This ... fit neatly into the Sumerians' mathematics and astronomic systems. This system is based on the numbers 6 and 60 which equal 360 when multiplied – the numbers are still used to divide the sky and every circular plane. No one knows why the Sumerians and later the Babylonians chose these numbers, though four thousand years later they remain the numeric basis for everything from determining ones position at sea to the location in the sky location of a distant galaxy vis-a-vis the earth.*"[5] Further, Babylonian records state that, "... *in the spring day and night are equal on the month Nisan; ....*" This means that an *equinox* occurred in the month Nisan, equivalent to our spring month of March, just as it does now. Their opening month was the month Nisan, a name used by the Jews when they returned to their land after their period of exile in Babylon. Nisan and the Jewish month Abib are equivalent months. From this the reader can immediately see the same description of the months and years described from Holy Scripture. "*Months of thirty days began with the light of the New Moon. How agreement with astronomical reality was effected, we do not know.*"[6] There was no evidence of intercalated days until, once again, in the seventh century B. C. when 5 days were added to the Babylonian year. Velikovsky[1] records of these additional days that, "*They were regarded as unpropitious, and the people had a superstitious awe of them.*" Does this "awe" point to the time when Berodachbaladan, the son of Baladan, king of Babylon, sent presents and letters to Hezekiah via his ambassadors "*Who (were) sent unto him to inquire of the wonder that was done in the land, ...*" (2 Chronicles 32:31)? Could they have been sent to learn about the miraculous changes in the astronomical conditions in the skies over Babylon and then adjusted their calendar accordingly? Also, recall that our modern calendar has its roots in the Babylonian calendar of the post seventh century era. How could the calendar be so much in error and then, over a short few centuries, suddenly completely change into one that fits the modern situation?

Ancient Assyria

In Assyria, the ancient year also consisted of 360 days. A decade of years was called a *sarus* with each *sarus* consisting of 3,600 days[5]. Note how different a *sarus* containing 365¼-day years would be. Assyrian months were 30 days each, counting from crescent to crescent[7-9]. Clay tablets from the royal library of Nineveh record the equinox at the 15th day of Nisan. Velikovsky records that, "*All the numerous data on solar movements in one of the systems lead to one and the same conclusion. The solstitial and equinoctial points of the ecliptic lay 6° too far to the east. The distances traveled by the Moon on the Chaldean ecliptic from one New Moon to the next are, according to Tablet No. 272, on the average 3° 14' too great. This means that during a lunar month the Moon moved a greater distance in relation to the fixed stars than present observation shows. In Tablet No. 32, the movement of the Sun along the zodiac is precisely calculated in degrees, and the station of the Sun at the beginning of each lunar month is determined exactly; but it is a perplexing presentation of the ununiform movement of the Sun. The question is insistent: why is it the Babylonians formulated the nonuniformity of the solar movement precisely in this way?*"[19]

Ancient Egypt

In Egypt, the ancient year was composed of 360 days. The first entry in Stein's *Kulturfahrplan*[16], under the Science, Technology, Growth section reads, "*The Egyptian calendar, regulated by Sun and Moon: 360 days, 12 months of 30 days each.*" Stein has this at between 5,000 B. C. and 4,000 B. C. The calendar of the Ebers Papyrus, from the New Kingdom, records a year of 12 months, 30 days each month.[10] Five *epagomena* days were added to the calendar at a later date. This change in the calendar was recorded in the Canopus Decree, containing both Egyptian and Greek languages. The Decree refers to the change as, "*the amendment of the faults of the heaven.*" Velikovsky[1] further records that "*the Ebers Papyrus shows that under the Eighteenth Dynasty the calendar had a year of 360 days divided into twelve months of thirty days each; other documents of this period also testify that the lunar month had thirty days, and that a New Moon was observed twelve times in a period of 360 days. The Sothis book says that this 360-Day year was established under Hyksos, who ruled after the end of the Middle Kingdom, preceding the Eighteenth Dynasty.*[17-18] *In the eighth or seventh century the five epagomena days were added to the year...*". Goudsmit[24] states: "*They (the Egyptians) also kept a separate year made up of 12 fixed 30-day months...Later, to make their lunar year jibe almost precisely with Sirius' rising, they tacked five extra days onto the year.*" Goudsmit states that the additional days were justified thusly: "*To account for them they created the myth of Nut, the sky goddess, who had been unfaithful to her husband, Re, the sun god. In retribution, Re decreed that she should bear a child 'in no month of no year.' But Nut's lover Thoth played dice with the moon and won five days a year. Because these days were outside the calendar, Re's decree did not apply. Nut's son was born on the first of them.*" Parise[23] records the time when the Egyptians made these adjustments: "*This 360 day calendar, like so many others, was changed during the 8th century B.C. to one of 365 days. The extra five days was simply added to the end of the year.*"

Ancient Rome

In ancient Rome, Plutarch[11] recorded that, in the time of Romulus, the Romans had a year of 360-days and recognized nothing else: "*During the reign of Romulus ...they only kept to the one rule that the whole course of the year contained three hundred and sixty days*". Numa–a contemporary of Hezekiah–attempted to reform the calendar to make up for the apparent confusion in the heavens. Plutarch[25] explains metaphorically what had occurred: "*Hermes playing at draughts with the moon, won from her the seventieth part of each of her periods of illumination, and from all the winnings he composed five days, and intercalated them as an addition to the 360 days.*" The explanation of this is as follows: a seventieth of twelve 30-day lunations yields five days and a fractional amount. This amount of time subtracted from the 360-day year results in a little more than 354 days, the same as twelve of our present lunar cycles. When added to 360, it is within a few hours of our current solar year length.[26]

Ancient Mayans, Mexicans and Peruvians

Velikovsky[1] provides evidence for the ancient 360-day year held by the Mayans, the Mexicans and the Peruvians. Later additions of 5¼ days are discussed.

Ancient China

The ancient Chinese had a 360-day year.[12-14] They also changed this to a 365¼-day year, calling the additional days *Khe-ying*.

Velikovsky[1] goes on to discuss the calendar reforms made at "*the end of the eighth or the beginning of the seventh century* B. C.". For example, Diogenes Laertius wrote in "*Life of Thales,*" "*He was the first to determine the Sun's course from solstice to solstice...He is said to have discovered the seasons of the year and to have divided it into 365 days...the first to predict eclipses of the Sun and to fix the solstices.*"[15] It is odd that this seventh century B. C. sage would be the *first* to fix the seasons. Why wouldn't it have been done earlier?

Our investigation has established that the records of these ancient civilizations record the occurrence of a 360-day year consisting of 12 months with 30 days per month. There is no evidence that they interpolated days anywhere in these various periods. Further, there is no evidence in the Bible anywhere that hours or days were to be inserted to make the month agree with the year. The addition of days was clearly a later (seventh century) change where 5 or 5¼ days were added to the calendar. Investigators acknowledge that sometime in the seventh or eighth century B. C. the old 360-day year calendar was modified.[23] Indeed, the scientific writings of these ancient civilizations describe detailed astronomical observations and detailed religious and civil activities based around a 360-day year. Why would they record such obviously different information on these ancient skies unless they were truly different than those we observe in times after the seventh century B. C.? Why would *all* of these civilizations–in some cases separated by many thousands of miles–record the exact same error?

Velikovsky's summary of the matter is of some importance to us: "*Scholars who investigated the calendars of the Incas of Peru and the Mayas of Yucatan wondered at the calendar of 360 days; so did the scholars who studied the calendars of the Egyptians, Persians, Hindus, Chaldeans, Assyrians, Hebrews, Chinese, Greeks, or Romans. Most of them, while debating the problem in their own field, did not suspect that the same problem turned up in the calendar of every nation of antiquity. Two matters appeared perplexing: a mistake of five and a quarter days in a year could certainly be traced, not only by astronomers, but even by analphabetic farmers, for in the short span of forty years–a period that a person could readily observe–the seasons would become displaced by more than two hundred days. The second perplexity concerns the length of the month.*" Medhurst[14] stated that, "*It seems to have been a prevailing opinion among the ancients that a lunation or a synodical month lasted thirty days.*" Velikovsky[1] goes on to say, "*Such declarations by ancient astronomers make it clear that there was no such thing as a conventional calendar with an admitted error; ..., the existence of an international calendar in those days was extremely unlikely. After centuries of open sea lanes and international exchange of ideas, no uniform calendar for the whole world has yet been devised: ...*"

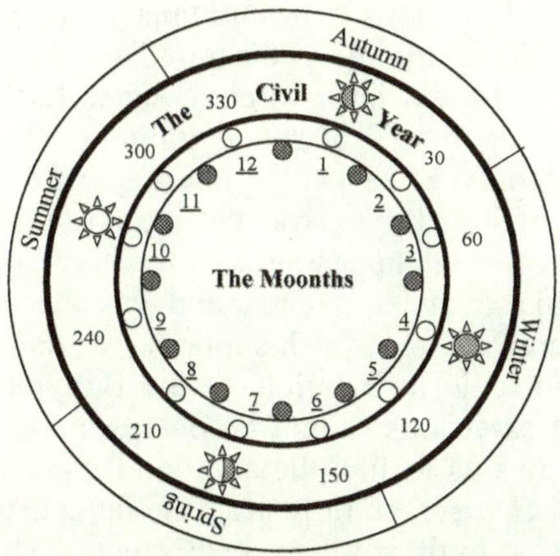

Summary

From the preceding biblical and historical evidence we can assemble a diagram that shows the critical elements of the 360-day year calendar. It is presented as a "clock" to emphasize the cyclical nature of the calendar. Unlike our present 365¼-day year calendar, the sun and moon's appearance throughout the year would have remained the same year after year. The center of the diagram shows the position of the New Moons (gray circles) and the Full Moons (white circles) during the year. Each month opens with the appearance of a New Moon.[1Y] At the twelve o'clock position, the months are numbered from one to twelve (underlined to distinguish them from days of the year). In Genesis, from the account of Noah, a similar convention is used. A month is recorded as simply "the fifth month" or "the seventh month." Different kingdoms at various times would come up with other naming conventions,

1 [Y] Alternatively any of the other Moon phases could be chosen – Crescent Moon, Half Moon, etc. We choose here the convention of the biblical record where the month opened with a New Moon

essentially no different than naming a month "July" or "September." The Full Moon's appearance occurred fifteen days after the appearance of the new moon, at the middle of the month. We can further state from biblical evidence that the New Moon and Full Moon appeared at our equivalent of six P. M. At the autumnal and spring (vernal) equinox this would be exactly at sunset for on this day there would be twelve hours of day and twelve hours of night, just as it is today.

Looking outward from the chart's center, we see four appearances of the sun in the ring entitled "The Civil Year." Civil activities have always been governed by the sun because of its complete control of the agricultural cycles. Looking just to the right of the twelve o'clock position is the symbol of a sun that is half gray, half white. This is the autumnal equinox. In the 360-day year the equinox occurred in the middle of the month (at the time of the appearance of the Full Moon). As we have already seen, Exodus 23:16 absolutely places the "*end of the year*"[23] at the beginning of the Feast of Ingathering. Morganstern records that the Feast of Ingathering was originally an equinoctial festival. The Feast of Ingathering was celebrated on the fifteenth day of the month (fifteen days after the appearance of the New Moon). Originally this was the first month in the Jewish calendar and was later changed to the seventh month by God's decree to Moses. This month was named Ethanim and later, after the return from exile in Babylon, to the Babylonian name Tisri. The importance of these assertions cannot be overestimated. This is the pivotal information that allows us to link the solar and lunar cycles of the 360-day year. Continuing clockwise, the fully gray sun depicts the winter solstice, the shortest day of the year in the northern hemisphere. This would occur ninety days later, or three months of thirty days each. Ninety days later than this we have the next half grayed sun depicting the spring (vernal) equinox. Many kingdoms used this as their year opening. Just as in the autumnal equinox, this occurred in the fifteenth day of the month and would coincide with a Full Moon. This also coincided with the Feast of the Passover when the Passover lamb was eaten. This was the month Abib in the Jewish calendar and later was changed to the month Nisan after the Babylonian month of the same name. Continuing clockwise, ninety days later, the summer solstice occurs (the longest day of the year in the northern hemisphere). Ninety days later we return to the top of the calendar clock and the cycle begins again. The sum of these days of the year is 360 days. In the calendar, a simple count, beginning at the autumnal equinox, shows how men living in these 360-day years would count off the year. Of course where the count began varied from kingdom to kingdom. The outermost ring contains the seasons. Each season, in the 360-day year, could be neatly assigned ninety days.

---

[23] The New Revised Standard Version is even more definite. It renders Exodus 23:16 as: "*... You shall observe the festival of ingathering at the end of the year. ...*"

It can be seen that the 360-day year was much simpler and more uniform than the calendars kept after the seventh century B. C. to measure the passage of time on earth simply during these early years. The question remains: how could this simple, uniform year of twelve months of thirty days per month change into the considerably more complex year we have today? This is the subject of the remainder of the book.

References

1. Velikovsky, Immanuel. *Worlds in Collision.* New York: Doubleday, 1950.
2. Thibaut, G. "Astronomie, Astrologie und Mathematik," *Grundriss der indo-artischen Philologie und Alterthumskunde* Strassberg: Verlag, 1899, III, 7.
3. Nyberg, H. S. "The Book of Denkart," *Texte zum mazdayasnischen Kalender*, Upsala, 1934.
4. Jeremias, A. "Das Alter der babylonischen Astronomie," 2nd Ed., Leipzig: J. C. Hinrichs'sche Buchhandlung, 1908.
5. Duncan, D. E.: *Calendar*, New York: Avon Books, Inc., pg. 14-5, 1998.
6. "Georgius Syncellus," ed. Jacob Goar, Paris, 1652.
7. Langdon, S. and Fotheringham, J. K.: *The Venus Tablets of Ammizaduga*, Oxford: Oxford University Press, 1928.
8. Johns, C. H. W.: *Assyrian Deeds and Documents*, IV, Cambridge: Deighton, Bell & Co., 1923.
9. Kohler, J. And Ungnad, A.: *Assyrische Rechtsurkunden*, Leipzig, 1915.
10. Legge, G.: *Recueil de travaux relatifs a la philologie et a l'archeologie egyptiennes et assyriennes*, Paris: Institut d'Egypte Cairo, 1909.
11. Plutarch: *Lives: The Life of Numa*, Vol. xviii, transl. J. Dryden, A.D. 75.
12. Scaliger, Joseph: *Opus de emendatione temporum* 1st Ed., Paris: 1583, 2nd Ed., Frankfurt, 1593; 3rd Ed., Leiden: 1598, 4th Ed., Geneva: 1629.
13. Hales, W.: *New Analysis of Chronology*, London: 1809.
14. Medhurst, W. H.: *The Shoo King*, transl., Shanghai: Mission Press, 1846.
15. Diogenes Laertius: *Lives of Eminent Philosophers*, transl. R. D. Hicks, Loeb, 1925.
16. Grun, Bernard: *The Timetables of History*, 3rd Ed., based on Werner Stein's *Kulturfahrplan*, Touchstone Books, 1991.
17. Von Bissing, F. W.: *Geschichte Aegyptens*, Weill: Chronologie egyptienne, 1904.
18. Kugler, F. X.: *Die babylonische Mondrechnung: Zwei Systeme der Chaldaer uber den Lauf des Mondes und der Sonne*, Freiburg im Breisgau, 1900.
19. Thomas, J.: *Eureka*, 3rd Ed., Walker, 1921.
20. Carter, W. H.: *Times and Seasons*, Birmingham, 1961.

21. Anderson, Robert: *The Coming Prince*, 12th Ed., London: Pickering and Inglis, 1929.
22. Parise, F.: *The Book of Calendars*, 2nd Ed., New Jersey: Georgias Press, 2002.
23. Goudsmit, S. A.: *Time*, New York: Time Incorporated, 1966.
24. Plutarch, *Isis and Osiris*, transl. by F.C. Babbit, Harvard: Harvard University Press, 1936.
25. Hollon, W., personal communication, 1999.
26. Morgenstern, J.: *The Gates of Righteousness*, Hebrew Union College Annual, VII, 1929.

"My days are like a shadow that declineth"

(Psalms 102:11)

YEAR OF THE MIRACLE-CHRONOLOGY OF THE REIGN OF HEZEKIAH

In this chapter, we look at chronology. The reader will recall that chronology requires us to fix events to a calendar. As long as whatever calendar system is used is fixed to astronomical observation and the immutable word of God, then we shall always be on firm ground.

We will begin by describing some of the events of the life of King Hezekiah. The Israelite Kingdom was split into two parts immediately after the reign of its third king, King Solomon. The northern kingdom was called Israel and the southern kingdom was called Judah. King Hezekiah lived in the eighth century B. C. while King Solomon the eleventh century B. C. He reigned over Judah. The Assyrians were now the dominant power in Mesopotamia and the Near East. Their inevitable push southward through the land of Israel would create the crisis which spawned the miracle that would affect us in this very day; the transformation of the yearly cycles themselves. We have shown that the year was previously made up of 360 days. At the closing moments of the eighth century B. C. this miraculous intervention by God in the affairs of man would cause the 365¼-day year that now frames the events of the lives of all those who live on this earth.

The Reign of Hezekiah

The reign of Hezekiah has many fascinating "coincidences" associated with it. Hezekiah's reign occurred after about 3000 years of history since the Adamic creation. In this sense, it occurred at the midpoint of God's 6000-year plan with the earth. The symbolic addition of fifteen years added fifteen years to his reign over Israel. This occurred at the midpoint of his reign.

The Bible states that Hezekiah reigned for twenty-nine years. Despite the political and military upheaval all around him, the southern Israelite kingdom of Judah flourished during his reign and Hezekiah created great wealth for Judah. Hezekiah was highly regarded by God and reformed many of the evil practices wrought by his father Ahaz and other previous kings[3§].

There are three accounts of Hezekiah's life in the Bible: in Kings, Chronicles and Isaiah. No other king's life is recorded in such a manner. The reader will find that a straightforward interpretation of events is made difficult by some apparently contradictory descriptions. The proper ordering of events in Hezekiah's life is a matter of some debate.

Chronology of the Period of the Miracle

We now have the task of determining the year in which the miracle of Hezekiah occurred. This requires a discussion of Bible chronology. Bible chronology is an exhaustive study (and very contentious). To get a flavor for the conflicting dates for biblical events, try searching for the date of a biblical event in the library or on the Internet. Note the wide range of dates for many of these events. Sometimes it is discouraging. For the non-expert, it is certainly confusing.

Our task is to get the year of the miracle on the sundial of Ahaz. We could analyze all of the events of the Bible, beginning with Adam, and march forward in time until we arrive at the time of Hezekiah's reign. Unfortunately, there are so many possible unanswered questions on the dates of biblical events that we could easily go astray. For sure, we would have little confidence in the final result.

But who says we have to go forward in time? Why not go backward in time? The advantage to this approach is this: after the miracle had occurred, the celestial motion of the moon and planets in our solar system followed a predictable course well-understood by scientists today. Knowing this we may use their methods with confidence up to the time of the miracle. This will be a great advantage because the science of calendar dating has been thoroughly examined and is well understood.

As we have previously discussed, scientific evidence has limitations. We believe the Bible contains the truth about historical events. However, we

3 [§] 2 Kings 18:2,4,7

need science to help us relate biblical events to a modern calendar; no way around that. Recall that the biblical justification for this is the directive given by God in Genesis 1:14: man is to use the movement of celestial objects such as the sun, moon, planets and stars to measure time on earth. As long as we stick with this principle, we can date biblical events with confidence. This is the important role astronomy–and the mathematics and physics of astronomy–has in helping us date events in a calendar. Astronomical methods allow us to move backwards and forwards in time and place events on a calendar of our choosing. That way all of the events are not only in proper order but they can be related to each other in terms of years, months, days, etc. We will select for our calendar dating method *universal time*. This is the time measured at Greenwich, England. Refer back to Chapter 2 for a more exact definition. When we refer to dates we will use the term "B.C." to equal a negative year in the universal time system plus one. Practically speaking that works like this: if the date of the occurrence of an event is, say, year -600 in the universal time system, then we will call it 601 B.C. so it can be related to a dating terminology more familiar to most readers. Just remember that the more "correct" way to express this year would be -600, not 601 B.C.

In biblical events after the miracle, there are some important considerations to achieve our goal. Here are some of them:

1. The reign of the kings of Israel ends during the reign of Hezekiah, king of Judah[4§]. This means that we cannot use the lengths of the parallel reigns of those kings to help us determine how to date events near the occurrence of the miracle on the sundial of Ahaz.
2. The reigns of the kings of Assyria, Babylon and Media-Persia are correlated to the events in Judah. For example, we learn that the first year of Nebuchadnezzar, king of Babylon, occurred during the fourth year of the reign of Jehoiakim, king of Judah. This is very valuable information for several reasons. Archaeology has revealed a great amount of information about the reigns of the Babylonian and Media-Persian kings (Nebuchadnezzar, Cyrus, Darius, etc.). They established empires that have been well-studied by historians. Of particular importance are archaeological discoveries in the late nineteenth and early twentieth century that provide astronomical information that allows us to date biblical events with high precision.
3. Significant world events can be correlated to biblical events. For example, the Battle of Carchemish, one of the most important

4 [§] E. Thiele[1] has the fall of the northern kingdom before the reign of Hezekiah begins. It is not the province of this book to refute or support this assertion. It is sufficient to say that during Hezekiah's reign, one can no longer use the duration of the reign of the kings of Israel to correlate the reign of the kings of Judah for the purposes of calendar dating.

battles in the history of the Mesopotamia, occurred during the fourth year of the reign of Jehoiakim, king of Judah.

4. Babylonian astronomers had a good understanding of the science of astronomy and their calendar dating is based on sound mathematical principles. Their astronomical observations allow us to use our advanced understanding to determine, with good precision, the days, months and years of chronological events.

Method of Dating the Time of the Miracle on the Dial of Ahaz–The Crossword Puzzle

We have established that we can use astronomy and the Bible to move backwards in time to date the year of the miracle. That means we are interested in biblical events that occurred after the miracle. Preferably we want an event that has lots of information that we can use to correlate to an astronomically determined date in the universal dating system calendar. But how do we do this in a manner that gives us very high confidence that we are correct?

Our method of choice is something like filling in a crossword puzzle. Crossword puzzles have rules. Words have a specific length. The first word must begin in the box marked for that question. Words go across or down, etc. Often there are some words that we have a very high level of confidence. Most people read all of the questions and try to pick the questions they can answer best. By filling in those boxes in the crossword puzzle we lock in place the letters of other words in which we are less confident. Letter boxes for words that occur across or down will share common letters. This provides a clue of what the undiscovered word might be and restricts the range of possible letters the word contains. Sometimes an entire word can be obtained by determining other words in the crossword puzzle. With a good strategy and a strong vocabulary, the puzzle is complete. The puzzle is "self-checking" in that if some words are out of place the puzzle cannot be completed properly. Alternatively, high confidence that the puzzle has been completed correctly is achieved when the definitions are answered correctly and all of the words fit together succinctly. This self-checking feature of crossword puzzles is very important. We will do the same as we date the year of the miracle. As we proceed, think of the crossword puzzle analogy; it's

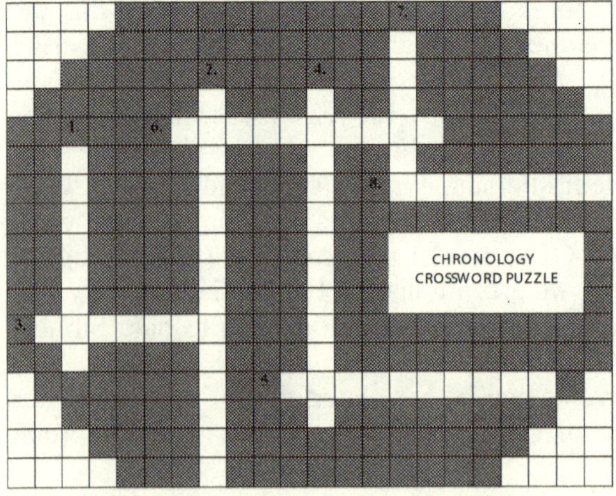

a good way to understand the dating methodology we'll be using.

We need to select a datable event that we have high confidence in. We choose the Bible and presume that the historical events it dates are the truth. Next, we want to link that date to our universal calendar. We will use astronomical methods to do this. We will correlate these discoveries to other events to convince ourselves that we are correct, just like a crossword puzzle.

First Step in the "Puzzle"–The 19th Year of King Nebuchadnezzar, King of Babylon, is the 11th Year of Zedekiah, King of Judah

We begin our "crossword puzzle" by going to the Bible. We select an important event after the miracle on the sundial of Ahaz. We are confident that one, important event in the Old Testament has a great deal of calendar information: the burning of the temple in Jerusalem.

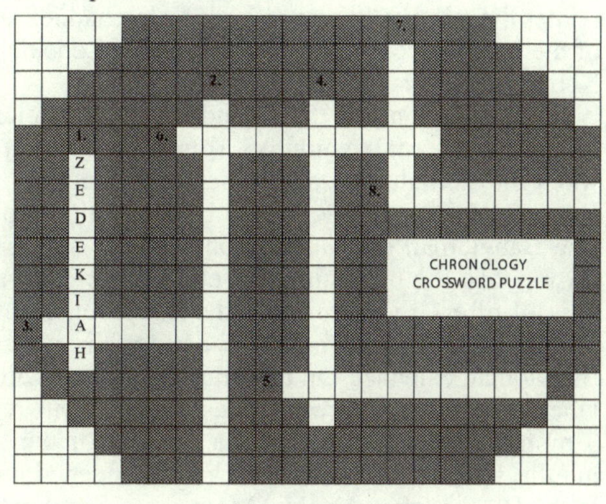

To set an historical context for this event, Babylon has established itself as the dominant power in the region. This began with Nabopolassar, king of Bablyon. The Babylonians, together with the Medes, ended the power of the Assyrian empire. Nabopolassar's son, crown prince Nebuchadnezzar, fought a decisive battle at Carchemish on the Euphrates against the Egyptian Pharaoh Necho. The Egyptians were defeated and the Neo-Babylonian Empire began.

Nabopolassar died and his son, Nebuchadnezzar, became king. He was enthroned in Babylon. He struck out to subdue the remnants of resistance to Babylon and this led him to Judah and its subjection in Nebuchadnezzar's first year of his reign. Years later, King Zedekiah–the last king of Judah–revolted and Nebuchadnezzar's army returned to Judah to overthrow the revolt. The prophet Jeremiah foretold this event and pleaded with his people not to resist the Babylonian army. They fought and lost, ending in the destruction of the city of Jerusalem and the temple of Solomon was burned and destroyed.

Here are some of the key biblical verses that refer to the event:
"*In the ninth year of Zedekiah king of Judah, in the tenth month, came Nebuchadrezzar king of Babylon and all his army against Jerusalem, and they besieged it. And in the eleventh year of Zedekiah, in the fourth month, the ninth day of the month, the city was broken up*" Jer. 39:1, 2.

"*So the city was besieged unto the eleventh year of king Zedekiah. And in the fourth month, in the ninth day of the month, the famine was sore in the city, so that there was no bread for the people of the land ... Now in the fifth month, in the tenth day of the month, which was the nineteenth year of Nebuchadrezzar king of Babylon, came Nebuzaradan, captain of the guard, which served the king of Babylon, into Jerusalem, And burned the house of the LORD, and the king's house; and all the houses of Jerusalem, and all the houses of the great men, burned he with fire*" Jer. 52: 5-6, 12-13.

A timeline illustration of this event is shown below. There are many important features to note. Of great importance is that we have an event that relates the reigns of the two kings; Nebuchadnezzar and Zedekiah. The burning of the temple occurred in the 11th year of Zedekiah's reign and the 19th year of Nebuchadnezzar's reign.

The beginning of the calendar year in ancient times was normally near the spring (vernal) equinox. You will recall that this is the time of year when the sunlight and nighttime were of equal length. This event was easily recognized by everyone. In the Bible the first month was referred to as Abib. The Babylonian equivalent month was Nisan. Using the Babylonian names for months, the beginning and end of a regnal year occurred in March/April (Nisan) of each year for both the Babylonians and the Judaic kings.[2] This is referred to as "Nisan-to-Nisan" dating. Nisan was also the first month of the Babylonian calendar. On the illustration, you will note hasher marks with the label "1/4." These represent one-quarter of one regnal year or, approximately, 3 months. We are told that the burning of the temple occurred in the fifth month, 10 days after a New Moon that opened that month. This must place it in the 10th day after the New Moon in August/September. This is reinforced by a reference that tells us that it was during the time of harvest (Jer. 40:10, 12).

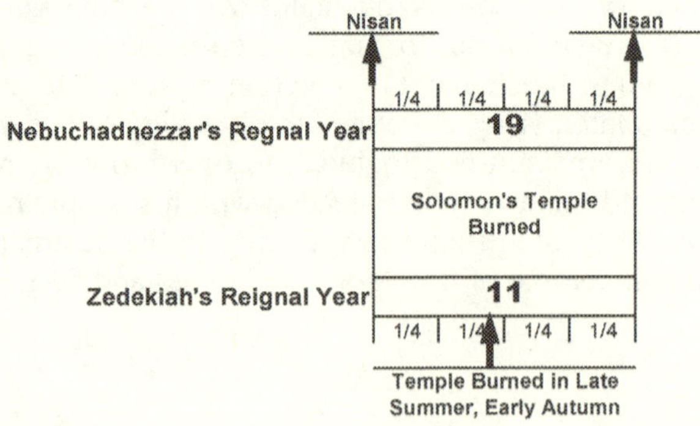

It can be seen that the calendar we have created satisfies almost all of our demands: it allows us to relate human events (the destruction of Solomon's temple) to an astronomical event (the Nisan-to-Nisan dating of the reign of the kings of Judah and Babylon).

Using our crossword puzzle analogy, if we are able to relate this event to other events through astronomical dating we can greatly reduce–perhaps virtually eliminate–any doubt about the dating of events. We are fortunate that sophisticated methods for calendar making were developed in this time period by some kingdoms that were more advanced in the mathematical sciences. In years prior to the miracle, calendar dating was simple under the 360-day year with 12 months of 30 days each system. The new, 365¼ day year caused discord between the lunar months and the solar year and new, more complex methods were required to keep time accurately. The Babylonians were exceptionally skilled in astronomy and mathematics. They were excellent timekeepers, even by modern standards. Archaeology in the nineteenth and twentieth centuries has uncovered substantial records kept by the Babylonians. Their principal writings were in cuneiform tablets. Their discovery and translation has yielded important information, including astronomical observations during the reign of king Nebuchadnezzar. That is the subject we will deal with next.

Second Step in the "Puzzle"–The 37th Year of King Nebuchadnezzar of Babylon

How will we get to a point where we have very high confidence that the date we determine for the miracle on the dial of Ahaz is correct? How will we relate the years of the reign of King Nebuchadnezzar and King Zedekiah to a modern calendar (and a time system we can investigate using astronomical sciences).

In the early twentieth century, German archaeologists discovered Babylonian cuneiform tablets containing astronomical observations throughout one of the years of king Nebuchadnezzar of Babylon. The day and month of the observation in the Babylonian calendar were noted. These astronomical observations came to be referred to as "Astronomical Diaries." One diary in particular was named "VAT 4956," according to the conventions of the scientists of that field.[3] The diary describes over thirty observations of the location of the planets relative

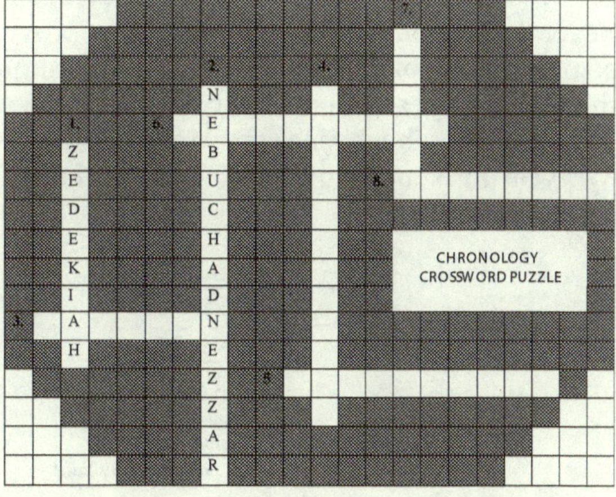

to the background of the stars and the earth's horizon. Weather conditions and other climatology information were also described. Most important, the writer states that he is describing the astronomical observations during the opening and closing of King Nebuchadnezzar of Babylon's 37th year of his reign. Recall that the first month of a Babylonian king's reign was Nisan. Here is a sample of the observations in the diary:

> "*Year 37 of Nebukadnezar, king of Babylon. Month I, (the first of which was identical with) the 30th (of the preceding month), the moon became visible behind the Bull of Heaven;...Saturn was in front of the Swallow...[The 11th] or 12th, Jupiter's acronychal rising...Month II...Saturn was in front of the Swallow; Mercury, which had set, was not yet visible...The 3rd, Mars entered Praesepe. The 5th, it went out (of it)...The 18th, Venus was balanced 1 cubit four fingers above a Leonis...Month III, (the 1st of which was identical with) the 30th (of the preceding month), the moon became visible behind Cancer...At that time, Mars and Mercury were 4 cubits in front of a [Leonis...] Mercury passed below Mars to the East; Jupiter was above a Scorpii; Venus was in the west opposite Z Leonis.*"[4]

The location of the planets and the moon are described relative to the stars and the Babylonian zodiac from the perspective of an observer in Babylon. The observations of the complete text are made throughout the year. It is interesting, anecdotally, that the writer of the diary notes many matter-of-fact items as well, such as the height of the water in the river ("*...the river level receded 8 fingers.*"), just as a diarist of any age might.

We cannot over-emphasize the importance of this discovery. Modern science can duplicate these conditions and determine the calendar period with good accuracy and precision. Astronomers have found that the opening period of the astronomical diary of VAT 4956 has the beginning and end of Nebuchadnezzar's 37th year are Nisan 1 for 568 and 567 B.C. respectively.

How likely is this correct? The relative location of the Moon and planets at an instant in time provides a unique description of the motion and position of these celestial objects that may not occur again for thousands of years. Several observations throughout a year provide a very precise description of astronomical conditions that are highly unique and may not be repeated for thousands of years. Such is the case with the astronomical observations of the 37th year of Nebuchadnezzar's reign. We may place high confidence that the 37th year of Nebuchadnezzar began in the spring, 568 B.C. and ended in the spring of 567 B.C.

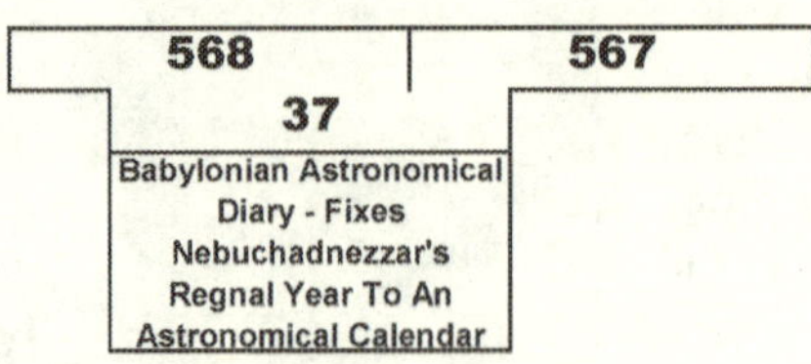

Third Step in the "Puzzle"–Dating the 19th Year of King Nebuchadnezzar, King of Babylon and the 11th Year of Zedekiah, King of Judah

The dating of the opening of Nebuchadnezzar's 37th year of reign can now be connected to the 19th year of his reign and this, in turn, fixes the 11th year of Zedekiah's reign. We have removed most of the years between the 19th of Nebuchadnezzar to the 37th of Nebuchadnezzar so the reader can see diagram clearly. By determining the date of the Babylonian King Nebuchadnezzar's 37th year we can state that the 11th year of King Zedekiah of Judah's reign was between the spring of 586 B.C. and the spring of 585 B.C. Again, the importance of this date cannot be overstated. We have connected a biblical date with a modern calendar.

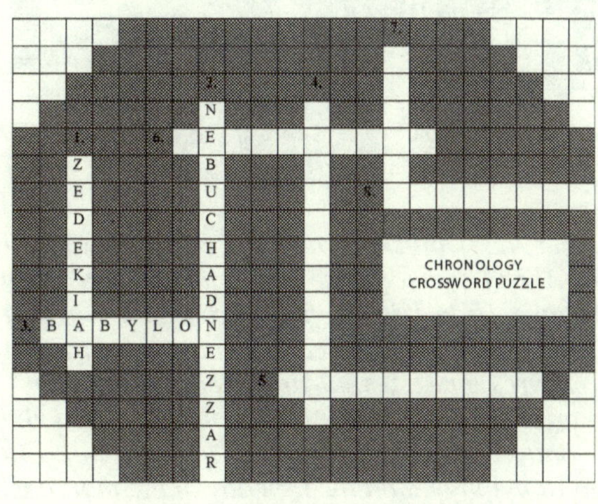

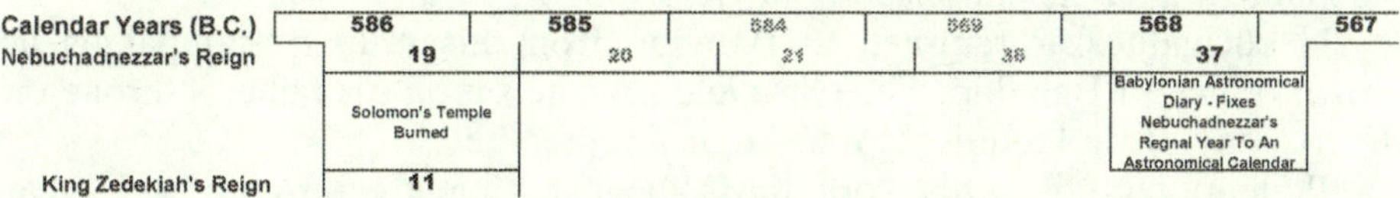

Can we further verify these date by additional information? Yes, we can.

Fourth Step in the "Puzzle"–The 5th Year of King Nabopolassar of Babylon

Nabopolassar was Nebuchadnezzar's father. Babylonian texts, referred to as the "Babylonian Chronicle," records the death of Nabopolassar and Nebuchadnezzar's accession to this father's throne in the 21st year of Nabopolassar's reign, as follows:

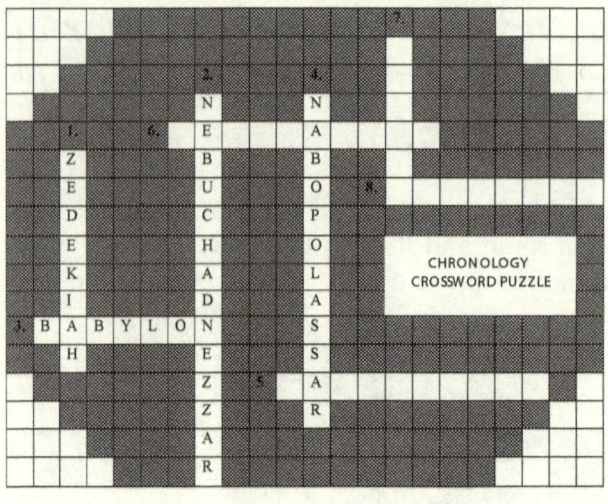

"[The 21st year]: The king of Akkad stayed home (while) Nebuchadnezzar (II), his eldest son (and) crown prince, mustered [the army of Akkad]. He took his army's lead and marched to Carchemish which is on the bank of the Euphrates. He crossed the river [to encounter the army of Egypt] which was encamped at Carchemish. [...] They did battle together. The army of Egypt retreated before him. He inflicted a [defeat] upon them (and) finished them off completely. In the district of Hamath the army of Akkad overtook the remainder of the army of [Egypt which] managed to escape [from] the defeat and which was not overcome. They (the army of Akkad) inflicted a defeat upon them (so that) a single (Egyptian) man [did not return] home. At that time Nebuchadnezzar (II) conquered all of Ha[ma]th. For twenty-one years Nabopolassar ruled Babylon. On the eighth day of the month Ab {month 5} he died. In the month Elul Nebuchadnezzar (II) returned to Babylon and on the first day of the month Elul he ascended the royal throne in Babylon. In (his) accession year Nebuchanezzar (II) returned to Hattu. Until the month Shebat he marched about victoriously in Hattu."[5]

Nebuchadnezzar returned to Babylon from his military campaigns as crown prince of Babylon. The chronicle says he sat on his father's throne on the first day of Elul (equivalent to August/September).

Ptolemy records in his work, the Almagest, a lunar eclipse in the 5th year of Nabopolassar's reign. He describes the characteristics of this lunar eclipse as follows:

"For in the year 5 of Nabopolassar (which is the year 127 of Nabonassar, Egyptianwise Athyr 27-28 at the end of the eleventh hour) the moon began to be eclipsed in Babylon[6]*." (The Almagest also records that no more than ¼ of the disk was obscured: a partial eclipse).*

Unfortunately, the use of lunar eclipse observations for biblical chronology is not as straight-forward as the Babylonian astronomical diary information we used to date the 37th year of Nebuchadnezzar. If you think about it lunar eclipses occur fairly frequently, astronomically speaking. For example, in 1982 A.D., there were three lunar eclipses. Simply recording that a lunar eclipse occurred in a particular year is insufficient to identify a year. It is true that the additional information provided by the Almagest (that it was Nabopolassar's 5th year, that it was a partial eclipse [less than one-quarter of the disk of the moon in shadow] and, of course, it occurred 11 hours after sunset) do make the event more specific. We also know it was the 5th year of Nabopollasar's reign.

However, we wish to set high standards for verification before we accept an idea. In particular, dates in the Almagest earlier than the sixth century B.C. have been disputed by physicist Robert Newton at Johns Hopkins University. We need to take a short digression to examine Newton's criticism of Ptolemy's Almagest before proceeding further with the dating of the lunar eclipse in the 5th year of Nabopolassar.

R. Newton's Dispute with Astronomical Data in the Almagest Prior to Sixth Century B.C.

As we have already mentioned, Ptolemy's Almagest was the work of Alexandrian astronomer Claudius Ptolemy. The Almagest is a highly regarded source of the chronology of antiquity. In it, Ptolemy developed a method for modeling the records of occurrences of eclipses made by ancient astronomers. Physicist Robert Newton investigated Ptolemy's Almagest to analyze some of the physical aspects of the slow changes to the celestial mechanics of the earth's orbit and rotation. Newton's objectives were scientific. Mathematical calculations of time must be adjusted for small fluctuations in the earth's rotation due to gravitational forces by other bodies in the solar system. Newton used the Almagest to try to understand these differences based on observations cataloged by Ptolemy. As a result of his studies, Newton eventually wrote a damning critique of Ptolemy's work, entitled, "The Crime of Claudius Ptolemy" in 1977.[7] Newton's controversial work has both its supporters and its critics. In Newton's defense, as a physicist, he approached Ptolemy's work from a different perspective than many of his predecessors (and critics), many of whom are historians. Of importance to us is that Newton and others showed that dates recorded in the Almagest after 600 B.C. are both accurate and reliable. In Newton's book, he stated that dates in the Almagest earlier than 600 B.C. are not reliable. But Newton relented somewhat on the 600 B.C. date in a response to an inquiry to a letter written by Carl Olof Jonsson in 1978:

"*I am not ready to be convinced that Ptolemy's king list is accurate before Nabopolassar [= before 625 BC], although I have high confidence that it is rather accurate for Nabopolassar and later kings.*"[8]

Our contention is that Newton is correct: Ptolemy's dating of the eclipses during the reign of kings prior to Nabopolassar recorded in the Almagest is incorrect earlier than the seventh century B.C. We must be careful to distinguish this assertion from the actual observations themselves as recorded by Ptolemy. Ptolemy extracted the observations from the Babylonian Chronicles; no doubt the observations are correct. However, one cannot apply his astronomical methodology to date eclipses prior to Nabopolassar's reign. This book explains why. The astronomical methods used for dating apply to a different orbit of both the earth and the moon than occurs after the miracle on the sundial of Ahaz during the 14th year of Hezekiah's reign.

Newton's support for Ptolemy's dating of the eclipse in Nabopolassar's 5th regnal year increases our confidence in using it for our dating of this Babylonian king's reign.

Verification of a Lunar Eclipse in the 5th Year of Nabopolassar, King of Babylon

By counting the years backwards from Nebuchadnezzar's 19th year of reign we encounter the year in which he ascended the throne after his father's death on the 8th of Ab(u), roughly August/September in our calendar. We have yet to explain the ascension year concept of Babylonian kings; that will explained later. But if we keep counting backwards from Nabopolassar's death in his 21st year or so to about 15 years earlier we arrive at the date of about 620-621 B.C. The question is: was there a partial lunar eclipse that occurred about this time?

Modern astronomical methods provide a means to verify eclipse observations. Meeus describes an algorithm for computing lunar eclipses. The algorithm is discussed in the appendix for the interested reader. The program shows that an eclipse occurs on April 22, 621 B.C. at the same time predicted by Ptolemy's Almagest. The characteristics are strikingly similar to his description extracted from the Babylonian Chronicle:

Description of the Eclipse	**Meeus' Astronomical Calculation**	**Ptolemy's Description, Based on Babylonian Chronicle**
Percentage of the Moon Darkened By The Eclipse	12% of the Moon Eclipsed	No More Than 25% of the Moon Eclipsed
Eclipse Time	Maximum Eclipse at About 6 AM	Eclipse began about 5:45 AM; Maximum Eclipse sometime later

April 22 is only a month after the vernal equinox where astronomical sunset would be near six PM local time. One month after the equinox would make sunset a little earlier but not greatly so. The "end of the eleventh hour" would be a little less than twelve hours after sunset. The match is very good. But are there other possible lunar eclipses before or after this eclipse that might also fit?

The table below lists the nearest possible eclipses (observable in Babylon) to the one on April 22, 621 B.C.

Before/After April 22, 621 B.C.	Meeus' Astronomical Calculation			
	Type of Eclipse	**Percentage of the Moon Eclipsed**	**Date of Maximum Eclipse**	**Time of Maximum Eclipse**
Before	Partial	54%	Sunday, December 6, 623 B.C.	8 PM
	Penumbral	39%	Thursday, October 27, 622 B.C.	10 PM
After	Total	100%	Sunday, October 6, 620 B.C.	1 AM

It can be seen that nearest partial eclipse is on December 6, 623 B.C. Note that over half the moon's disk is in shadow in that eclipse: surely this is not the right one. Although there is apparently some evidence that the Babylonians recorded penumbral eclipses, it is unlikely that this is the eclipse referred to by Ptolemy. After April 22, 621 B.C. the next observable eclipse was on October 6, 620 B.C. and it was a total eclipse. Surely this is not the correct one either. None of these eclipses are near the time the eclipse is said to have occurred except for the one recorded on April 22, 621 B.C. We may therefore date the 5th year of Nabopolassar's reign from Nisan 1 (March/April), 621 B.C. through Nisan 1 (March/April), 620 B.C.

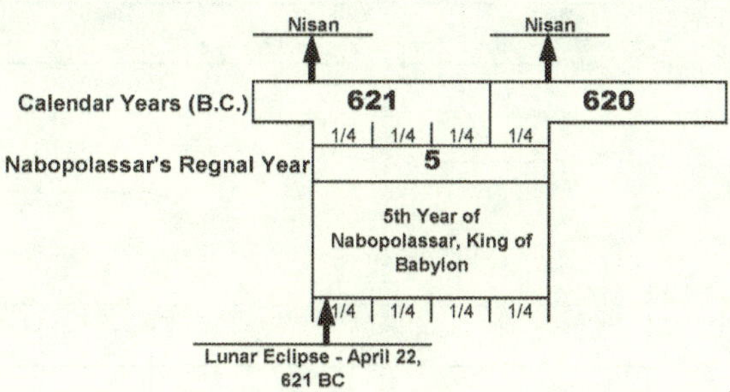

Fifth Step in the "Puzzle"–Dating of the Accession Year of Nebuchadnezzar, King of Babylon and the 4th Year of Jehoiakim, King of Judah

The preceding dating of the 5th year of Nabopolassar is similar to writing down a word in our crossword puzzle that we are somewhat confident in but would like to have that extra assurance that it is correct. We have high confidence in the 19th year of Nebuchadnezzar (and the 11th year of Zedekiah).

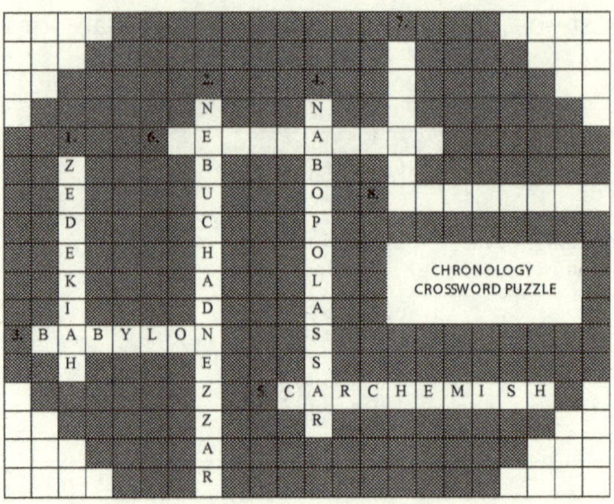

By correlating these two dates we will meet in the middle at another important date.

By going forward in time from the date of the 5th of Nabopolassar and backward in time from the 19th of Nebuchadnezzar, we arrive at the beginning of Nebuchadnezzar's reign and the 4th year of Jehoiakim somewhere in the middle. Note that we have pinned two dates earlier and later than this date with very strong evidence that does not allow us to stray more than a few months. This should give us high confidence in dating the important 4th year of Jehoiakim.

Unfortunately, our puzzle is a little more complex now. First, unlike before, we have moved outside the reign of the king of Babylon (Nebuchadnezzar) and into the reign of another (Nabopolassar). Second, we have also moved from the reign of Zedekiah backward through the reigns of Jehoiachin and into the reign of Jehoiakim, king of Judah. What's more, we will discover that Jehoiachin reigned for only 3 months and 10 days.

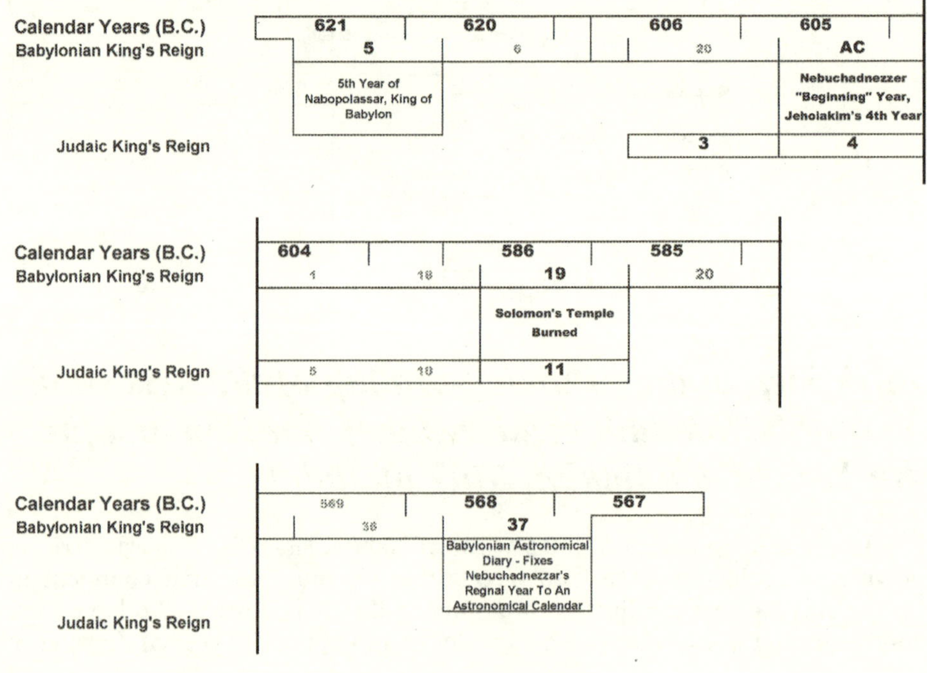

In keeping with our theme of leaving complex issues for the appendix, we leave the discussion of connecting the 4th year of Jehoiakim, king of Judah to the accession year of Nebuchadnezzar, king of Babylon for that part of the book.

The diagram shows the chronological fit. The 4th year of Jehoiakim was from Nisan 1, 605 B.C. through Nisan 1, 604 B.C.

Sixth Step in the "Puzzle"–The Remarkable "Lock" Provided By the Prophet Ezekial

We have seen from Step One and Step Three that the destruction of the temple was on August/September 586 B.C. We have determined that date by dating the 37th year of Nebuchadnezzar's reign in Step Two from the Astronomical Diary and from the 5th year of Nabopolassar reign in Step Four. Now we have attempted to determine the 4th year of Jehoiakim (which, it turns out, was the accession year of Nebuchadnezzar). We found this to be 605 B.C., the same year as the battle of Carchemish. The Bible narrative forces us to date the reign of king Jehoiachin as his reign was between the reigns of Jehoiakim and Zedekiah. He reigned for a short 3 months and 10 days. It seems odd that the Bible would be so specific about the day.

The prophet Ezekial records two remarkable prophecies that ties together the destruction of Jerusalem, the burning of the temple and the 2 Ki. 24:12 captivity of Jehoiachin and his servants. His prophecy locks together our interpretation. It is very similar, once again, to a crossword puzzle where the discovery of one word fits all of the other words that have been filled in, leaving no doubt that the puzzle has been correctly solved!

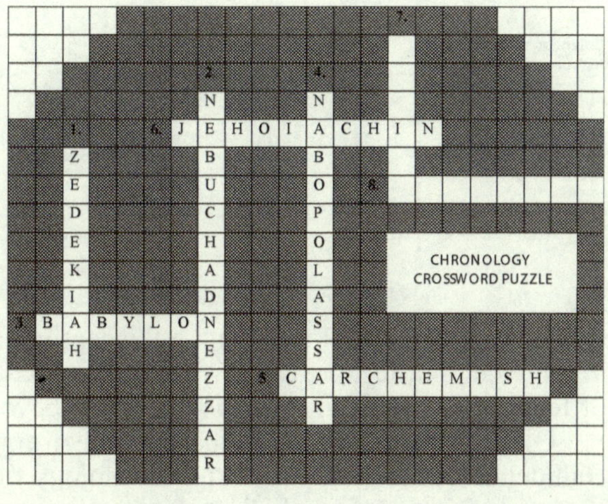

The first reference by Ezekial is given in Chapter 33:

"*And it came to pass in the twelfth year of our captivity, in the tenth month, in the fifth day of the month, that one that had escaped out of Jerusalem came unto me, saying, The city is smitten.*" (Eze. 33:21)

The second reference occurs in a vision in Ezekial 40:1:

"*In the five and twentieth year of our captivity, in the beginning of the year, in the tenth day of the month, in the fourteenth year after that the city was smitten, in the selfsame day the hand of the LORD was upon me, and brought me thither*" (Ezek. 40:1)

What is "the captivity" referred to by Ezekial? Clearly it is the same event. Ezekial 33 is referring to the same destruction of the city we investigated in Step One. We know that the city was "smitten" in August/September, or, the 5th month in the 10th day of the month, in 586 B.C. Ezekiel was told about 4 months later. Twelve years earlier would be 597 B.C., the accession year of Zedekiah and the year when Jehoiachin was taken into captivity in Babylon. The beginning of the year of Ezekial's 25th year of captivity would be March/ April 573 B.C. This would be in the 14th year after the destruction of the temple.

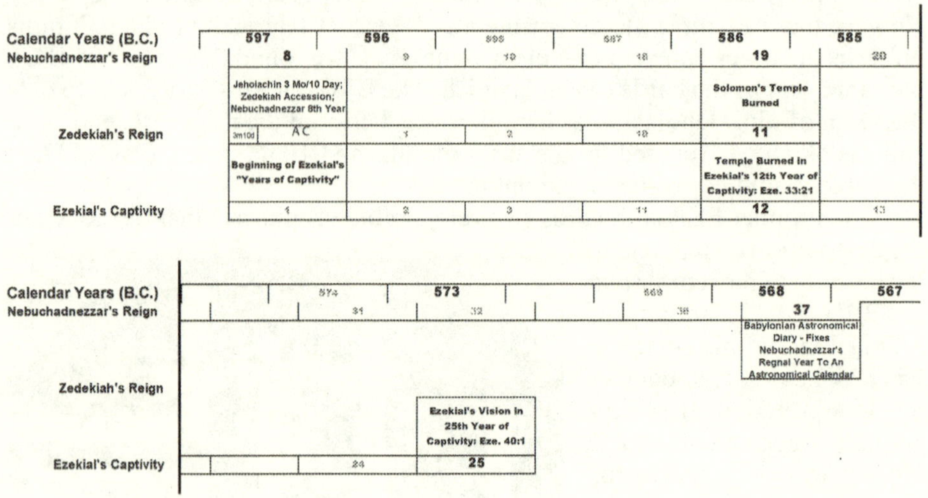

Therefore, Ezekiel was among the captives during the exile of Jehoiachin to Babylon. A little more effort would undoubtedly allow us to date the very day of Jehoiachin's exile to Babylon but that is beyond the intent of this book.

Of importance to us is that we have confirmed to a high degree of confidence the correctness of the chronology of reigns of the kings of Judah from Jehoiakim to Zedekiah and the reigns of the kings of Babylon from Nabopolassar to Nebuchadnezzar.

Seventh Step in the "Puzzle"–The Leap Back to the 13th Year of the Reign of King Josiah

CHRONOLOGY CROSSWORD PUZZLE

We must now rely on the certainty we have achieved from the interlocking chronologies of the kings of Judah and Babylon and the astronomical information we have that provides us with a direct way to connect their reigns to a modern calendar. Our single source for counting backwards to the miracle on the sundial of Ahaz is the Bible. The prophet Jeremiah provides us with a way to skip from the 4th of Jehoiakim to the 13th year of the reign of King Josiah:

"The word that came to Jeremiah concerning all the people of Judah in the fourth year of Jehoiakim the son of Josiah king of Judah, that was the first year of Nebuchadrezzar king of Babylon; The which Jeremiah the prophet spake unto all the people of Judah, and to all the inhabitants of Jerusalem, saying, From the thirteenth year of Josiah the son of Amon king of Judah, even unto this day, that is the three and twentieth year, the word of the LORD hath come unto me, and I have spoken unto you, rising early and speaking; but ye have not hearkened." (Jer. 25:1-3)

Since we know that the 4th year of Jehoiakim's reign was from March/April 605 B.C. through March/April 604 B.C. from Step Five, Jeremiah's prophecy allows us to leap back 23 years to the 13th of Josiah. Josiah's 13th regnal year must be March/April, 628 B.C. through March/April, 627 B.C.

Eighth Step in the "Puzzle"–Counting Backwards To the Year of the Miracle on the Sundial of Ahaz

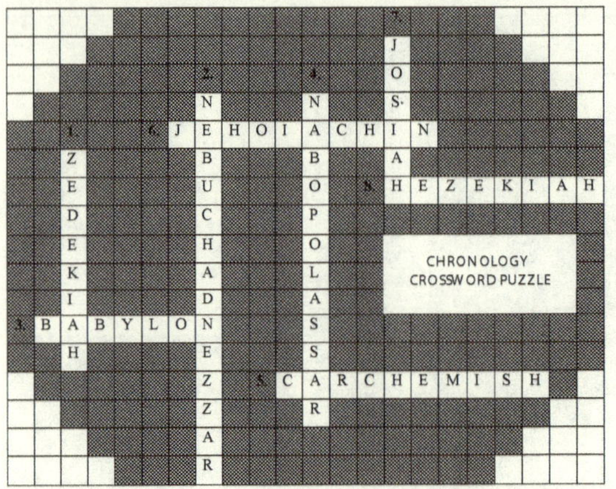

The scriptures record the reigns of the kings of Judah after the death of King Hezekiah. We know that, from the date of the miracle, 15 years were added to Hezekiah's life. It is particularly important to identify the month and year of Manasseh's accession.

King of Judah	Scriptural Reference	Duration of Reign	Month of Reign	Years of Reign
Josiah's 13th Year	Jer. 25:3	13	March/April	628 B.C. - 627 B.C.
Josiah's Accession	Jer. 25:3	-	March/April	641 B.C.
Amon	2 Ki. 21:18	2	March/April	643 B.C. - 641 B.C.
Manasseh	2 Chr. 33:1	55	March/April	698 B.C. - 643 B.C.
King Hezekiah	**Scriptural Reference**	**Years Before Manasseh's Accession**	**Month of Reign**	**Year of Miracle**
Miracle	Isa. 38:5	15	March/April	713 B.C.

Ussher's Date For The Miracle

Finally, it is worth noting that the biblical chronologist Ussher[9] determined the same year, 713 B. C., as the date of the miracle on the sundial of Ahaz. Ussher did not have access to either the astronomical or the archaeological evidence we have today. Nevertheless, his dating of the miracle on the sundial of Ahaz has been confirmed by later biblical chronology using the new discoveries.[1]

This provides some additional confidence in our results.

The Miraculous Going Down of the Sun on the Dial of Ahaz

We are now ready to investigate the miracle itself. The full explanation has been left to the appendices. There the reader will find a complete revealing of the methods that were used to uncover this great mystery. It is recommended that the reader immediately turn to the appendices once this subsection has been read.

The proposition is made that, previous to the going down of the shadow on the sundial of Ahaz, the civil timekeeping of the earth was governed by a 360-Day yearly orbit consisting of 12 30-day months. We affirm the numerous astronomical observations made by kingdoms throughout the earth prior to the miracle as being correct. At that time, *there was complete accord between cycles of the Sun and Moon.* We propose that the going down of the shadow was caused by a shift in the Sun's position retrograde to the natural rotation of the earth to cause the reversal of the shadow[5bb]. This change caused the earth to alter its orbit from a 360-Day orbit to a 365¼-day orbit. This change also affected the moon's orbit, causing it to change from a 30-day orbit to 29½ days. The Moon and Sun were no longer in phase and a new, more complex lunisolar cycle emerged. The day, month and year were no longer simple multiples of each other. The detailed description of how this change occurred can be found in the appendices. It will be found to be in complete accord with the scriptural record. A summary of what happened is detailed below:

1. The orbit of the earth around the sun was, prior to 713 B. C., a circular (eccentricity of zero) 360-Day orbit with uniform angular velocity and a constant radial position vector (relative to the solar system barycenter),
2. The Lord miraculously caused the sun to move from its position at the barycenter of the Solar System, adjusting the position and velocities of all the orbiting planets,
3. On the earth, this movement of the sun appeared on the sundial of Ahaz to cause the shadow on the dial to recede 10°,
4. From that instant forward, the new orbit of the earth was slightly elliptical and the new year was no longer 360 days in length but was now approximately 365¼ days; the orbital angular velocity now changing throughout the year with a constantly changing radial position vector,
5. The new orbit has the same orbital characteristics as we observe today (except for the slow, predictable variations well known to astronomers).

The day that the miracle occurred can be determined from the orbital position of the Earth in the new 365¼-day orbit. With the simulation method used, only one of two seasons of the year is possible. One of the seasons puts the time of the miracle in late summer or late winter of 713 B. C

5 [bb] An alternative explanation is that God miraculously moved the earth itself[2]. This is dealt with in the appendix where the computer simulation is discussed.

An interesting question the reader may ask: "What day of the year was it in the old, 360-Day year calendar"? The question cannot be answered from the astronomical investigation and can be supplied only by inference from the bible. It would appear to be reasonable that there was a 15-day advance in the new calendar from the old with a net difference of 10 days when the 5¼-Day increase in the year's length was considered. This was the 15 days – a day for a year – promised to Hezekiah as a sign.

The Season of the Year When the Miracle Occurred

There is good evidence for the Sun going down on the dial as being in winter or early spring. There was a time of year when the kings of Mesopotamia would go to battle: ***"And it came to pass, after the year was expired, at the time when kings go forth to battle, that David sent Joab, and his servants with him, and all Israel; and they destroyed the children of Ammon, and besieged Rabbah. ..."*** (2 Sam. 11:1). The *expiry of the year* was during the month Ethanim, the Jews' Civil Year: "***...the feast of ingathering, which is in the end of the year,***" (Exod. 23:16). The *expiry of the year* and *the end of the year* was one and the same time; the 15th day of the month Ethanim, equivalent to our month of September. The time when kings went to battle, then, would be late winter or early spring.

Other evidence points to the season for the siege of Jerusalem being in late winter or early spring. At that time, the Rabshakeh, one of Sennacherib's representatives said: ***"Thus saith Sennacherib king of Assyria, Whereon do ye trust, that ye abide in the siege in Jerusalem? Doth not Hezekiah persuade you to give over yourselves to die by famine and by thirst,..."*** (2 Chronicles 32:10-11). His confidence that they would die of thirst must have come from his knowledge that the Jews had stopped the fountains and streams in the country (v. 3), probably to prevent poisoning by the Assyrians and to ruin the land so the occupying forces would not benefit. But what about famine? It must mean that it was at a time of the year when they would have no stores of food, exhausted by months of consuming food harvested in the late summer months. This clearly points to late winter or early spring. In a later chapter astronomical evidence will show that the time of the year of the miracle was early spring.

This would make the day of the miracle: February 10, 713 B.C. Ussher[9] has the date of the miracle in the spring of 713 B.C.[6Π].

6 Π Pg. 82. Ussher designates this as year 3291 AM and 713 BC. He uses the letter "c" to represent the time of the year. "c" represents the spring season.

Sun Dial Design

The form of the sundial is not known for certain. Our evidence for it is implied by 2 Kings 16:10-11:

"And king Ahaz went to Damascus to meet Tiglathpileser king of Assyria, and saw an altar that was at Damascus: and king Ahaz sent to Urijah the priest the fashion of the altar, and the pattern of it, according to all the workmanship thereof. And Urijah the priest built an altar according to all that king Ahaz had sent from Damascus: so Urijah the priest made it against king Ahaz came from Damascus."

Whilst we could assume that this altar was also a sundial (as this was the common practice at the time), we cannot say for certain. However, what *is* certain is that the design of the dial would follow the pattern common to design principles of this era. It was certainly not a design provided by the God of Israel.

However, an interesting confirmation of the results can be made concerning the nature of the sundial. All sundials, of whatever design, have common bases for their construction. It has been proposed that sundial design at the time preceded the discovery of the necessity to point the gnomon in the direction of the north celestial pole in order to obtain true hour angle changes.[10] The style common at this time had the dial directed toward north so the sun in the southern sky would cast its shadow and allow proper measurement. The weakness of this older method of hour angle measurement was that *if the dial were relocated to a different longitude it would not record correct hour angles*. Determining true north was easily accomplished and was a well-established practice at this time. Damascus is approximately 1° longitude farther east of Jerusalem. Assuming the design was copied in detail, and ***"... the pattern of it, according to all the workmanship thereof"*** was properly duplicated, the hour angles for a sundial set for Damascus would not work properly and would be slightly different as well. The angle of arc in the sky necessary to create the effect of 10° on the dial of Ahaz is computed to be 10.954°. The difference of approximately 1° in longitude and perhaps the particular design differences in the proper hour angle because the dial's gnomon was not pointed at the north celestial pole.

References

1. Thiele, E. R.: *The Mysterious Numbers of the Hebrew Kings*, Grand Rapids, MI: Kregel Publications, 1983.
2. Jones, F. N. *Chronology of the Old Testament: A Return to Basics*. 15th Ed., Green Forest, AR: Master Books, 2004.
3. Neugebauer, P.V. and Weidner, E.F.: *Berichte über die Verhandlungen der Königlich Sächsischen Gesellschaft der Wissenschaften* 67 (2)", pgs. 29–89, 1915.
4. Sachs, A. & Hunger, H.: *Astronomical Diaries and Related Texts from Babylonia*, Vol. I, Vienna: 1988.
5. Grayson, A. K.: *Assyrian and Babylonian Chronicles*, Texts from Cuneiform Sources, A. L. Oppenheim, et al., Ed., Locust Valley, NY: J. J. Augustin, 1975.
6. Ptolemy, Claudius: *The Almagest*, Great Books of the Western World, Chicago: William Benton Pub., Book 5, pg. 172, 1952.
7. Newton, R. R.: *The Crime of Claudius Ptolemy*, Baltimore: Johns Hopkins University Press, 1977.
8. Newton, R. R.: Response to a Letter from Jonsson, C. O., Aug., 1978.
9. Ussher, J.: *Annals of the World*, transl. , L. & M. Pierce, L. & M., Green Forest, AR: Master Books, 2003.
10. Mayall, R.N. and Mayall, M. W.: *Sundials: How to Know, Use, and Make Them*, Cambridge, MA: Sky Publishing Corp., 1973.

"For the invisible things of him from the creation of the world are clearly seen, being understood by the things that are made, even his eternal power and Godhead; so that they are without excuse:" (Romans 1:20)

6

DIVINE PURPOSE BEHIND THE CHANGE IN THE LENGTH OF THE CIVIL YEAR

By changing the length of the year, God has left an indelible mark on man's affairs for all time. This mark is experienced by all men for all experience in their daily lives the effect of the motion of the Earth, moon and the apparent motion of the sun as time marches forward. The worldwide flood that killed all of mankind except Noah and his family, the miraculous crossing of the enslaved Hebrews across the Red Sea, the resurrection of Jesus Christ; all can be relegated to the mists of antiquity and can be dismissed for lack of "proof." The clear evidence for change in time itself cannot. For the non-believer, this presents quite a challenge. No natural phenomenon can be attributed to the changing of the orbit of the earth and moon around the sun. No comet, planetary perturbation due to a "near passage" or atmospheric refraction model can be used to explain why, suddenly, in the seventh century B. C., there is the addition of 5¼ days to an earlier year of 360 days. Immanuel Velikovsky, his work quoted extensively in Chapter 4, undoubtedly understood this principle clearly. Let us, once and for all, put an end to the silly notion that these ancient peoples could not properly measure the length of the year. It is the hope of the author that a more fruitful branch of serious investigation will emerge for what competent scholars already know; that these people possessed significant skill in measuring astronomical events and creating precise calendars. We have simply lacked the knowledge to understand the astronomical conditions of their time.

The "discovery" that the ancient year was comprised of 360 days is, of course, not new. Prior to the seventh century this fact would have been commonly known. It has been found by those who study ancient chronology. Unfortunately, their works are often reported in scholarly journals and consequently their findings are not commonly known. Worst, some proposed the unsatisfactory explanation that these ancient people were unable to fix the number of days in a year accurately. It is easy to show that this explanation is absurd. It would be a trivial thing for intelligent men of all ages to fix the number of days in a year. That these ancient people would all make the same mistake cannot be explained. A 360-day year was proposed by Velikovsky and others. Their explanation for a change to the year we have today was based on natural causes: close approaches by other planets, asteroids, etc. These explanations have been successfully refuted by scientists.

Bible students are often tempted to explain biblical miracles by natural causes. As for the miracle of the going down of the shadow on the sundial of Ahaz, some Bible students have explained this miracle by fabricating imaginary sundials or supposing that God miraculously changed the position or source of light on the sundial of Ahaz: the so-called Shekhinah or, God's glorious radiance. Ussher's explanation was probably the best of all: that he could not explain how but that it did happen! However, even the great chronologist Ussher falls short here as he goes on to say that no change in the time systems of the earth resulted from this miracle.

The surprise is that the explanations of these two, great enigmas are directly related to each other. There WAS a 360-day year prior to the seventh century B.C. and up to the midpoint of Hezekiah's reign. The position of the sun DID miraculously return along the arc in the sky it had already traced from sunrise to the point in time later in the morning when the miracle occurred, yielding a 10° decline on the Syrian imported sundial by Hezekiah's father, Ahaz. The world's time clock–both sun and moon–were thereafter changed due to the effects of gravity on their orbit. The year lengthened and the month shortened.

The Biblicist has been kept from understanding this miracle because of a lack of satisfactory (scientific) explanation. The scientist has been kept from understanding how the length of the solar year could change by the requirement he believe in a miracle caused by the God of the Bible.

The whole world has been left with an indelible mark of God's intervention in the civil affairs of men. Christian apologetics can be ignored or explained away by anti-Christian skeptics through various philosophical arguments well-known to those who study them. The evidence of God's design in nature–a Christian fable once thought to be forever destroyed by Darwin's natural selection proposition–has been successfully renewed due to glaring holes in the evolution argument. Yet the evolutionists can still continue in hope that a new philosophy will explain the incongruence in Darwin's theory. But an unexplained change in the orbit of the earth and moon around the sun cannot be explained by any possible physical means. If the length of the year DID change then only God could have accomplished it. God demonstrates once again that He can change the affairs of man and even the measuring stick of time of those affairs.

If the reader is convinced that the earth once had a 360-day year then this book explains how it changed. But why did it change and why have we come to know it at this time? Part of the answer is that a scientific explanation requires the use of numerical methods to model the physics of the miracle, requiring relatively advanced understanding of the motion of masses. A thorough investigation is realized through use of a digital computer; a development of the latter part of the twentieth century. This has kept the solution hidden for the many centuries since being first discovered, apparently, by the Babylonians who visited Hezekiah after recovery from his illness. Somehow they came to understand that his recovery and the change in the length of the year were related.

Why now? The author believes that God is about to intervene in this world in ways the world has never seen. We cannot say when, for the day and the hour are not known. The author cannot say it will be in one year or ten. But relative to the course of man's history, it will be proportionally a very short time, probably within a generation. If you accept the evidence presented you must also accept that the God of Abraham, Isaac and Jacob and the heavenly Father of Jesus Christ has done it. Perhaps this evidence of God's power, hidden and now revealed, will yet convince the non-Christian man or woman that he should find out more about this great God before it is too late and these world-changing events begin.

APPENDIX 'A'
CALCULATING THE TIME OF THE EQUINOXES IN THE 365¼-DAY YEAR

Meeus[1] provides a calculation for the March and September equinox. Y is the year (in astronomical Ephemeris Years where Astronomical Years = -B. C. Years + 1) and y = Y/1000.

March Equinox

$$JD = 1721139.2855 + 365.2421376Y + 0.0679190y^2 - 0.0027879y^3$$

September Equinox

$$JD = 1721325.6978 + 365.2425055Y - 0.1266890y^2 + 0.0019401y^3$$

Where JD = Julian Days. Julian Days are converted to calendar days using formulae presented elsewhere in the appendices.

The results of this calculation will show that there are not an equal number of days between the time interval after the March equinox and before the September equinox and the time interval after the September equinox and before the March equinox. This is because of the ellipticity of the barycenter of the earth-moon orbit around the sun resulting in a changing radial and tangential velocities of the barycenter relative to the much more constant diurnal rotation of the earth on its axis.

References

1. Meeus, J.: *Astronomical Formulae for Calculators,* 4th Ed., Richmond, VA: Wilmann-Bell Inc., 1988.

APPENDIX 'B'
CALCULATING THE TIME OF THE LUNAR PHASES IN THE 365¼-DAY YEAR

The motion of the moon in its monthly orbit around the center of mass of the earth-moon system is highly complex. The average distance of the earth to the moon is approximately 384,400 km. The moon's orbit is inclined relative to the ecliptic at an angle of 5°.1453964 (see, for example, Taff[1]). The eccentricity of the orbit is 0.054900489, considerably greater than the eccentricity of the earth's orbit around the sun. The sidereal period of the moon is $27^{d}.321661 = 27^{d}07^{h}43^{m}11^{s}.5$. This is referred to as the "astronomical" cycle of the moon. It is not used in the Bible.

In the present day orbit, the period of time from a complete cycle of phases is about $29^{d}.53059$ and is referred to as a *synodic period*. This is the proper time period used to measure the length of time of the cyclic phases of the moon. However, these phases are out of sync with the solar cycle so the New Moon occurs at various days of the calendar month. Calendars based on the synodic period yield year cycles far less than the present 365¼-day solar period and intercalation is required to rectify the two time systems. In the fifth century B. C., the Greek philosopher Meton observed that the moon and sun are in phase over a 19-year solar period. The complete cycle is referred to as a Metonic cycle. Its principal value lies in the investigation of the long-term synchronicity of the sun and moon time systems in historical investigations. Despite the apparent difficulty of the use of the moon's periodic motion of a time measuring instrument, Taff[1] observed that, *"...the Moon has the largest geocentric motion of any natural body in the solar system, in practice it is more accurate and expeditious to use observations of the Moon rather than those of the Sun or the planets."* It is an interesting observation that demonstrates the wisdom of God's choice of the moon as the Divine time-piece to measure the feasts of the Israelites.

As explained in the main text, the Jewish calendar was always based on the appearance of the New Moon. It marked the beginning of months. The modern Jewish calendar uses the "astronomical" New Moon as the instant of the beginning of the month. The astronomical New Moon is when the earth, moon and sun are all in a straight line in space. They are said to be "in conjunction." Ancient peoples could not observe conjunction because the brightness of the sun prevents direct observations of this epoch and so methods based on direct observation have always been somewhat inaccurate after the seventh century B. C.

Celestial mechanics has long struggled with modeling the motion of the moon. For example, it is known that its relative closeness to the earth requires one to take account of the non-uniform distribution of mass in the earth to obtain precise results. Another is that the sun's gravity greatly affects the motion. Newton himself struggled to obtain a proper model of the moon's motion. It is beyond the scope of this book to attempt to model the motion of the moon.

Brahde[3] computed moon phase tables from 601 B. C. to A. D. 2700 using the mathematical solutions of Brown and Newcomb. He used 1-day time steps in his numerical analysis and computation. These solutions require the inclusion of a large number of terms of a harmonic series that Brahde truncated to obtain accuracy to within 1 minute of arc. Discussions of this theory can be found in the works, for example, of Brouwer and Clemence[4] or Taff. The uncertainty is how to convert Ephemeris Time (E. T.) (which is used as the independent variable in the mathematical equations employed by Brahde) to Universal Time (U. T.) (based on solar time used in civil timekeeping). There is an unpredictable small, annual change in the rotation rate of the earth on its axis of fractions of a minute. Over a long period of time, it is believed that the rotation of the earth has slowed. These small, annual differences can result in differences of hours when investigating historical events dating back to the seventh century B. C. The conversion from E. T. to U. T. is discussed elsewhere in the appendices. Brahde used an "improved" conversion method in his book based on work by R. Newton. Newton based his conversion on ancient eclipse records.

Meeus[2] provides a calculation for the timing of the lunar phases and it is his calculation method used in this book. The computation steps are:

Step 1–The Julian day is computed for the appearance of the New Moon and the Full Moon from the equation:

$$JD = 2415020.75933 + 29.53058868k + 0.0001178T^2 - 0.000000155T^3 + 0.00033 \sin(166^\circ.56 + 132^\circ.87T - 0^\circ.009173T^2)$$

Where k is:

$$k = int[\,(year - 1900) \times 12.3685\,]$$

And "year" is the astronomical year, which is the B. C. year plus 1. A. D. years remain unchanged. For example, the B. C. year 713 is–712 astronomical year. The year is input as a fraction. For example, midyear would be –712.5. The nearest integer value is taken to obtain the final answer for k. The value for the New Moon uses k = k + 0.0 whereas for a Full Moon k = k + 0.5.

T is the time in Julian centuries from January 0.5, 1900 E. T. and is approximated by:

$T = k/1236.85$

Step 2–The sun's mean anomaly (M), the moon's mean anomaly (M') and the moon's argument of latitude (F) are determined at JD:

$$M = 359°.2242 + 29°.10535608k - 0°.0000333T^2 - 0°.00000347T^3$$

$$M' = 306°.0253 + 385°.81691806k + 0°.0107306T^2 + 0°.00001236T^3$$

$$F = 21°.2964 + 390°.67050646k - 0°.0016528T^2 - 0°.00000239T^3$$

Step 3–A correction is made to the JD using M, M' and F:

Corrected JD = JD + (0.1734 – 0.000393T) sin M + 0.0032 sin (2M) - 0.4068 sin (M') + 0.0161 sin (2M') – 0.0004 sin (3M') + 0.0104 sin (2F) – 0.0051 sin (M+M') – 0.0074 sin (M-M') + 0.0004 sin (2F+M) – 0.0004 sin (2F-M) – 0.0006 sin (2F+M) + 0.0010 sin (2F-M) + 0.0005 sin (M+2M')

Step 4–The result is converted into U. T. and the formula 15° longitude = 1 hr. is used to compute local time (in the case of Jerusalem, 35°13' 00" E longitude means that $2^h.348$ is added to the U. T.).

Step 5–The result from Step 4 is converted to calendar time.

The results were compared to Brahde's tables. For example, Brahde predicts an astronomical New Moon on October $19^d18^h1^m$ U. T., 601 B. C. Using Meeus' calculations (the computation method used in this book), we obtain the following:

U. T. = E. T. - ΔT = October $19^d.936$ – $4^h.701$ = October $19^d17^h46^m$, a difference of 15 minutes.

Brahde also predicts a Full Moon on Nov. $4^d4^h28^m$ U. T., 601 B. C. Meeus' calculations predict:

U.T. = November $4^d.373$ – $4^h.701$ = November $4^d4^h15^m$ U. T., a difference of 13 minutes.

Meeus' calculation of modern Moon phases differs by no more than 2 minutes with most being less than 1 minute when compared to the Astronomical Ephemerides.

The favorable comparison between Brahde's results (using advanced numerical methods and corrected using eclipse tables from archaeological evidence) and those obtained through use of Meeus' method gives confidence in using the proposed method for computing the time of the Full Moon and the New Moon in the seventh century B. C.

References

1. Taff, L. G.: *Celestial Mechanics: A Computational Guide for the Practitioner*, New York: John Wiley & Sons Inc., 1985.
2. Meeus, J.: *Astronomical Formulae for Calculators*, 4th Ed., Richmond, VA: Wilmann-Bell Inc., 1988.
3. Brahde, R.: *Moon Tables : Phases of the Moon, for Times Past, Present, and Future, 601 B.C-2700 A.D.= Brahdes Maanetabellar*, Oslo: Nordanger forl, 1974.
4. Brouwer, D., Clemence, G. M.: *Methods of Celestial Mechanics*, New York & London: Academic Press, 1961.

APPENDIX 'C'
CALCULATING THE TIME OF LUNAR ECLIPSES IN THE 365¼-DAY YEAR

An eclipse occurs is when the shadow cast by the earth is seen on the face of the moon. A full moon is observed when the earth is between the sun and the moon. The moon's complex motion around the center of gravity between the earth-moon system, as mentioned elsewhere, does not remain within the ecliptic but strays in access of 5°. Consequently, a full moon whose face is not obscured by the earth shadow is observed much more frequently. A lunar eclipse is observed only when the moon crosses the ecliptic and when the moon is full.

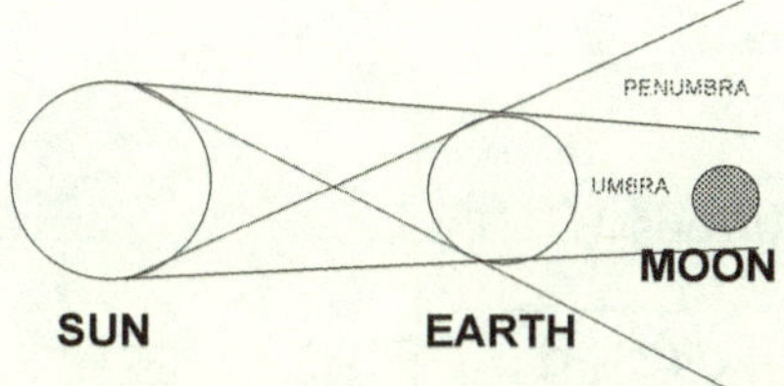

Meeus[1] once again supplies us with the method for determining the critical parameters of the eclipse and, in particular, the time of the maximum eclipse. The algorithm he recommends computes both umbral and penumbral eclipses. It is unlikely that penumbral eclipses were used much in the time period of interest. Of the umbral eclipses, both partial and total eclipses are both detected. The steps used in the program that was created are:

Step 1–Get a start date. Determine the time and date of the next full moon computer routine calculates the same factors used in the lunar phase computation, described elsewhere in the appendices.

Step 2–Taking the moon's argument of latitude, F, solve the following inequality:

$|\sin F| > 0.36$

If the answer is "true," then there is no eclipse. The program skips to the next months and tests this full moon event. If the answer is "false," then there is an eclipse.

Step 3–For an eclipse event, the time of maximum eclipse and other eclipse factors are calculated (see Meeus' book for details). The eclipse magnitude is determined from the equations:

$$\textit{penumbral magnitude} = \frac{1.5572 + u - |g|}{0.5450}$$

$$\textit{umbral magnitude} = \frac{1.0129 - u - |g|}{0.5450}$$

The formulae for u and γ are in Meeus' book. If the umbral magnitude is negative, there is no umbral eclipse and the eclipse is penumbral.

Step 4–If the eclipse is umbral it can be either partial or total. The semidurations are determined in ephemeris minutes as:

$$P = 1.0129 - u$$

$$T = 0.4679 - u$$

$$n = 0.5458 + 0.0400 \cos M'$$

$$\textit{partial phase} = \frac{\theta}{n}\sqrt{P^2 - g^2}$$

$$\textit{total phase} = \frac{\theta}{n}\sqrt{T^2 - g^2}$$

The routine was tested against cases provided by Meeus in his book. Recent cases were tested against NASA eclipse data. In all cases, acceptable accuracy was obtained for the purpose of testing Ptolemy's eclipse observations.

References

1. Meeus, J.: *Astronomical Formulae for Calculators*, 4th Ed., Richmond, VA: Wilmann-Bell Inc., 1988.

APPENDIX 'D'
CALCULATING THE TIME OF THE PERIHELION PASSAGE IN THE 365¼-DAY YEAR

Meeus[1] provides a calculation for the perihelion passage. The Julian day (JD) is computed from:

$$JD = 2415021.546 + 365.2596413k + 0.0000000152k^2$$

where k is:

$$k = int\,[0.99997\,(year - 1900)]$$

And the year is the decimal fraction of the year in the ephemeris time scale. The Julian days are then converted to calendar days using methods described also by Meeus.

Meeus' calculation is particularly well suited to the numerical part of this investigation because the time of the passage is the time of passage of the earth-moon barycenter. The numerical calculations are based on ephemeris days from perihelion passage of the earth-moon barycenter. Therefore, the values given by Meeus' calculations were taken absolutely as the calendar time of the perihelion passage in 702 B. C. and the value determined from the numerical study was added to it to give the date and time when the miraculous event occurred. However, it also points out the limits to the approximations used by assuming that the earth-moon center of mass is the same as the time of the observer's true crossing of a vernal point on the earth:

1. The center of mass of the earth-moon system is 4728 km from the center of the earth or about ¾ of the way to the surface.[2] As Meeus points out, the greatest and least separation distances between the earth and moon might introduce errors in the order of one day when this barycentric calculation is used,
2. Planetary perturbations can introduce some error in the calculation and, to be more correct, these planetary perturbations should be considered.

These corrections necessary for determining the exact moment when the miracle occurred was not deemed essential to the numerical investigation. The forward progress in time of the equinoxes–the true beginning and ending of the year–is much more important.

A further and future investigation into determining the orbital transfer of the moon and its present 29½-day synodic period from the older 30-day period is desirable.

References

1. Meeus, J.: *Astronomical Formulae for Calculators*, 4th Ed., Richmond, VA: Wilmann-Bell Inc., 1988.

APPENDIX 'E'
CALCULATION OF THE LENGTH OF THE YEAR

The Tropical Year

The biblical method for determining the length of the year was from equinox to equinox. This is called the tropical year.

The post 360-Day tropical year is given, for example, by Taff[1]. It is computed from the equation:

$$\text{Tropical Year} = 365^d05^h48^m45^s.0 - 0^s.530T_E = 365^d.24219878 - 6^d.14 \times 10^{-6}T_E$$

Where T_E is measured in Julian centuries of 36,525 days from Jan. $0^d.5$, 1900 E. T. "E. T." is "Ephemeris Time." Ephemeris Time is the invariant, uniform time that is the independent variable in the Newtonian equations of motion.

The Sidereal Year

The sidereal year is the time interval for one complete revolution of the earth around the sun relative to the fixed stars. We refer to the stars as "fixed" because their distance relative to the average distance in the solar system is so great, they are considered to be fixed:

$$\text{Sidereal Year} = 365^d06^h09^m09^s.5 + 0^s.01T_E = 365^d.25636042 + 1^d.1 \times 10^{-7}T_E$$

The Anomalistic Year

The anomalistic year is the time interval from perihelion to perihelion. The perihelion is the point of the earth's elliptic orbit around the sun when the earth is closest to the sun. It can be determined from:

Anomalistic Year = $365^d06^h13^m53^s.0 + 0^s.26T_E = 365^d.25964134 + 3^d.04 \times 10^{-6}T_E$

The question of why the sidereal year is longer than the tropical year can be answered by noting the following diagram. If an observer notes the location of a particular star along the horizon and, one day later, notes the time it takes to return to exactly the same azimuth location (transit) he will note that this period differs from doing the same observation for the sun. The reason is that the stars are fixed in the sky and hence their transit is based on the diurnal rotation of the earth on its axis. However, for the sun transit, it moves its apparent position relative to the earth because of the earth's orbit around the sun (a change in location of approximately 0°.0986 per day over the orbit). This makes the day based on observing the stars (a "sidereal day") $23^h56^m4.1^s$ in mean solar time, slightly less than a solar day. Hence a sidereal year composed of these shorter days is slightly longer. The Bible uses the time from equinox to equinox so biblical solar time is always based on the tropical year, not on the sidereal year. The primary benefit of the sidereal year is in performing certain numerical calculations based on the earth's orbit around the sun.

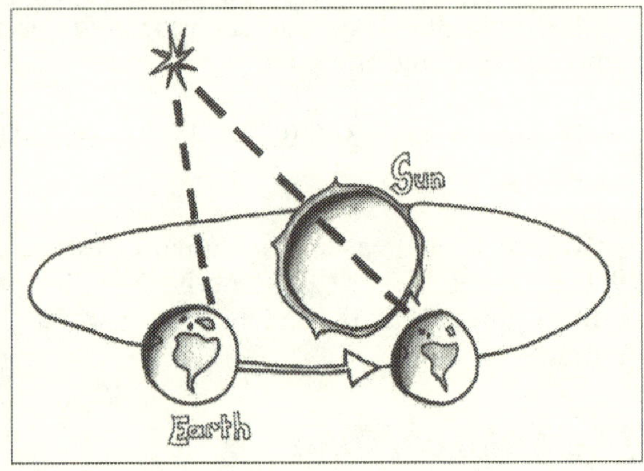

Reference

1. Taff, L. G.: *Celestial Mechanics: A Computational Guide for the Practitioner*, Hoboken: John Wiley & Sons Inc., 1985.

APPENDIX 'F'
CALCULATION OF UNIVERSAL TIME FROM EPHEMERIS TIME

Ephemeris time is the independent variable in the equations of motion of celestial bodies. For example, it is the independent variable in Newton's equations that govern the motion of the mass in the Solar System. Universal time is based on the rotation of the earth and, hence, is the time system used to govern civil life. Universal time is the time computed for Greenwich, England. Various methods are employed to convert Universal Time to local time (time at various locations throughout the earth). Meeus[1] provides the following equation for making the conversion of Ephemeris Time (ET) to Universal Time (UT):

$$UT = ET - \Delta T$$

Exact differences between UT and ET can be determined only from observation. However, for times in the seventh century B. C., an approximate formula can be used:

$$\Delta T = 0.41 + 1.2053T + 0.4992T^2$$

and T is the time in centuries from 1900 and ΔT is in minutes. Dates before A.D. 1900 makes T a negative value.

Reference

1. 1. Meeus, J.: *Astronomical Formulae for Calculators*, 4th Ed., Richmond, VA: Wilmann-Bell Inc., 1988.

APPENDIX 'G'

DERIVATION OF THE EQUATIONS OF MOTION

Newton's law of gravitation is that all mass in the universe attracts every other mass with equal and opposite force in proportion to the mass' values. The force due to gravitation between two bodies (A and B) can be determined. Using the nomenclature of Brouwer and Clemence, [5]

$$F = \frac{k^2 m_A m_B}{r^2}$$

Where F is the force, m is the mass of the body, r is the separation distance between the two bodies and k is the universal gravitational constant. The orbital motion of the earth around the sun is assumed to occur on a plane called the ecliptic. This allows us to look only at the two-dimensional aspects of this problem. Further, we assume that the two bodies that are moving under mutual gravitation are the sun (denoted S) and the center of mass of the earth and moon (denoted EM). The equations of motion relate the mass and acceleration of the bodies to the force where

$$m_{EM}\ddot{\xi}_{EM} = k^2 m_{EM} m_S \frac{\xi_S - \xi_{EM}}{r^3}$$

$$m_{EM}\ddot{\eta}_{EM} = k^2 m_{EM} m_S \frac{\eta_S - \eta_{EM}}{r^3}$$

$$m_S\ddot{\xi}_S = k^2 m_{EM} m_S \frac{\xi_{EM} - \xi_S}{r^3}$$

$$m_S\ddot{\eta}_S = k^2 m_{EM} m_S \frac{\eta_{EM} - \eta_S}{r^3}$$

And where,

$$m_{EM}\ddot{\xi}_{EM} + m_S\ddot{\xi}_S = 0$$

$$m_{EM}\ddot{\eta}_{EM} + m_S\ddot{\eta}_S = 0$$

This is the component version of the famous Newtonian relation F = ma where 'a' is acceleration. The position unit vectors (ξ,η) are used to denote an orthogonal, Euclidean reference frame. We use the dot and double dot components to represent the first and second order derivatives, respectively, of the position with respect to time.

These equations are often called the equations of motion of the center of mass. Their practical consequences are that at the center of mass the net forces are equally balanced. It also shows why the gravitational forces of stars and superior planets can sometimes be ignored. It further shows why bodies with small relative masses can be treated as if the point of origin is at the primary body. For example, the sun contains 98.8% of the mass of the solar system. While the center of mass of the solar system– referred to as the barycenter of the two bodies–has a slight displacement from the heliocenter of the sun, it can be ignored to obtain errors of $O(10^{-8})$. In the case of the earth and moon, the moon's mass is 1:38,900 that of the earth. The net effect is that choosing the center of mass at the earth's geocenter is correct to distances of $O(10^{-5})$.

We are interested in the relative motion of the earth-moon center of mass to that of the sun. The equations can be manipulated to achieve this by making the following transformation,

$$x = \xi_{EM} - \xi_S$$
$$y = \eta_{EM} - \eta_S$$
$$r^2 = x^2 + y^2$$
$$\mu = k^2 (m_{EM} + m_S)$$

The resulting equations are,

$$\ddot{x} = -\mu \frac{x}{r^3}$$
$$\ddot{y} = -\mu \frac{y}{r^3}$$

It is these equations that are solved to determine the position of the earth-moon barycenter. As an aside, all other planets, moons (collectively "point masses") in the solar system can be included to determine the motion under mutual gravitation using Cowell's[3] method. Using the subscript j to refer to the jth planet in the solar system, simultaneous consideration of all of the planets (and moons) can be considered using the relation:

$$\ddot{x} = -k^2(1+m_{EM})\frac{x}{r^3} + \sum_j k^2 m_j \left(\frac{x_j - x}{\rho_j^3} - \frac{x_j}{r_j^3} \right)$$

$$\ddot{y} = -k^2(1+m_{EM})\frac{y}{r^3} + \sum_j k^2 m_j \left(\frac{y_j - y}{\rho_j^3} - \frac{y_j}{r_j^3} \right)$$

The mass of the sun is set equal to 1 and all other masses (denoted by the subscript j) are made relative to the sun's mass.

Under certain assumptions, and if there are only two masses to be considered, the motion can be solved analytically. This approach was used in modeling the effect of the movement of the sun on the sundial of Ahaz. Refer to elsewhere in the Appendix for the principles behind the application of the method.

For motion in a plane, four initial values in velocity and position are required. These initial values were determined using Kepler's 3rd law for a 360-day year. The numerical integration method used is called the 4th-order Runge-Kutta[4] method. Integration of the acceleration terms leads to the velocity and position. Numerical integration of the second order equations of orbital motion are called initial value problems.

References

1. Cowell, P. H., Crommelin, A. C. D. "Investigations of the motion of Halley's Comet from 1759-1910," Appendix to *Greenwich Observations 1909*, Neill, Bellevue, England, 1910.
2. *Numerical Recipes in FORTRAN 77: The Art of Scientific Computing*, Cambridge: Cambridge University Press, 1986.

APPENDIX 'H'
NUMERICAL APPROXIMATION USING THE 4TH-ORDER RUNGE-KUTTA METHOD

In order for us to solve the equations of motion in celestial mechanics, we have seen that the general form of these equations cannot be solved directly and, necessarily, we must resort to (approximate) numerical methods to solve them. This can be accomplished in many different ways. A discussion of the Runge-Kutta method employed in the simulation of the sun's movement will be made below. We will show the development of the numerical principles of the approach and then address the issues of approximation error.

Runge-Kutta numerical integration methods are commonly referred to as "one-step" methods. This considerably simplifies the start conditions for initial value problems such as the present case. Numerical methods based on Taylor series expansion, like the so-called predictor-corrector methods, require the determination of position and velocity at several start positions in order that the higher order derivatives can be included in the finite difference calculations. Typically this would require about ten position and velocity components to be known *a priori*.

The Runge-Kutta method, while using a predictor-corrector-like approach, achieves the equivalent of using finite difference methods with higher order derivatives but requires only the determination of lower order derivatives. The simulation of the sun's movement and the resulting perturbation of the earth-moon barycenter has been modeled using the 4th order Runge-Kutta method (meaning equivalent to 4th-order precision of a Taylor expansion). However, the algebra required to obtain the result is extensive so the 2nd-order algorithm will be described only and the discussion will then extrapolate to the 4th-order method.

A simple extrapolation can be obtained for each time step in an integration by the following equations for two-dimensional, planar motion:

$$\dot{x}_{i+1} = \dot{x}_i + \Delta t\, \ddot{x}_i$$

In words, this equation says that we can determine the new x-component of the velocity of the earth-moon barycenter at the i+1th time step by multiplying the instantaneous acceleration (determined by Newton's equations) at the time step i by a chosen finite time step Δt and adding this result to the original position to determine the velocity component in the x-direction at the new position. We can write three additional equations that allow the determination of the y-component of the velocity vector and the x and y position:

$$\dot{y}_{i+1} = \dot{y}_i + \Delta t\, \ddot{y}_i$$
$$x_{i+1} = x_i + \Delta t\, \dot{x}_i$$
$$y_{i+1} = y_i + \Delta t\, \dot{y}_i$$

For the remainder of the discussion we will show the relationship between the x-component of the velocity vector and its derivative, the x-component of the acceleration, only but the same form of the equation will equally implied for the remaining three equations required to determine the earth-moon barycenter's position and velocity at each timestep as the simulation proceeds.

The 2nd-order Runge-Kutta method derivation begins by considering the sum of a weighted average of two time evaluations of the x-component of the acceleration:

$$\dot{x}_{i+1} = \dot{x}_i + \Delta t(a\, k_1 + b\, k_2)$$

The derivatives k_1 and k_2 are chosen such that,

$$k_1 = \ddot{x}_i$$
$$k_2 = \dot{x}_i + q\Delta t\, \ddot{x}_i = \dot{x}_i + q\Delta t\, k_1$$

where q is a constant value yet to be determined. After considerable manipulation it is found that,

$$\dot{x}_{i+1} = \dot{x}_i + \frac{\Delta t}{2}(\ddot{x}_i + \bar{\ddot{x}}_{i+1})$$
$$\bar{\ddot{x}}_{i+1} = \dot{x}_i + \Delta t\, \ddot{x}_i$$

This method is called the improved Euler's method. The overbar signifies an intermediate calculation of the derivative. This intermediate step is regarded as a predictor step. A trial approximation is obtained and then the computation is corrected using the corrector step.

Higher order methods are more complex extensions of this approach. A 4th-order method involves three intermediate steps for each timestep used by the model. The simulator used in our simulation uses the relation,

$$\dot{x}_{i+1} = \dot{x}_i + \Delta t(a\,k_1 + b\,k_2 + c\,k_3 + d\,k_4)$$

In practice, the acceleration (due to gravitation) is a function of both mass and separation distance. Therefore the k_1, k_2, k_3 and k_4 derivatives are computed for both position and velocity simultaneously. The algorithm steps are as follows:

Step 1–The initial position and velocity are known at the origin of each timestep Δt (including the start position). We designate the start x-component conditions (remembering that there is an equivalent and parallel set of y-component calculations) as:

$$\begin{aligned} &\textit{Position}: \quad x_i^{(1)} \\ &\textit{Velocity}: \quad \dot{x}_i^{(1)} \\ &\textit{Acceleration}: \quad \ddot{x}_i^{(1)} \end{aligned}$$

The superscript "(1)" designates this as the first of four initial and intermediate approximations that, together, will comprise the final integration. The subscript "i" indicates that this is the ith timestep. We will advance one timestep to compute the position and velocity at the i+1th timestep that, in turn, becomes the start conditions for the next timestep. We begin the assembling of the derivatives by computing k_1:

$$\begin{aligned} k_1' &= x_i^{(1)} + \Delta t\, \dot{x}_i^{(1)} = x_i^{(2)} \\ k_1'' &= \dot{x}_i^{(1)} + \Delta t\, \ddot{x}_i^{(1)} = \dot{x}_i^{(2)} \\ \ddot{x}_i^{(2)} &= \ddot{x}_i^{(2)}\left(x_i^{(2)}\right) \end{aligned}$$

The superscript “"“ represent derivatives of the velocity (acceleration) and “‘“ represents derivatives of the position (velocity). Therefore k_1'' is the acceleration at the beginning of present ith timestep. The acceleration of the Earth-Moon barycenter around the Sun is computed from,

$$\ddot{x}_i = -\mu \frac{\xi_{E-M} - \xi_S}{\rho^3}$$

where ξ is the x-component of the Sun (S) or Earth-Moon barycenter (E-M) position. At the outset of the simulation, $\xi_S = 0$. When the sun is miraculously moved, $\xi_S \neq 0$ and is some finite value. The constant μ is a function of the relative masses of the sun and the combined masses of earth and moon and the square of the universal gravitational constant. It is discussed further in the main text. ρ is the separation distance between the sun and the earth-moon barycenter,

Step 2–We now must compute the position, velocity and acceleration at an intermediate location as specified by the 4th-order Runge-Kutta method for the intermediate derivative k_2. There are two "k_2" values to determine for both the position and velocity:

$$k_2' = x_i^{(2)} + \frac{\Delta t}{2}\dot{x}_i^{(2)} = x_i^{(3)}$$
$$k_2'' = \dot{x}_i^{(2)} + \frac{\Delta t}{2}\ddot{x}_i^{(2)} = \dot{x}_i^{(3)}$$
$$\ddot{x}_i^{(3)} = \ddot{x}_i^{(3)}\left(x_i^{(3)}\right)$$

Step 3–Compute k_3:

$$k_3' = x_i^{(3)} + \frac{\Delta t}{2}\dot{x}_i^{(3)} = x_i^{(4)}$$
$$k_3'' = \dot{x}_i^{(3)} + \frac{\Delta t}{2}\ddot{x}_i^{(3)} = \dot{x}_i^{(4)}$$
$$\ddot{x}_i^{(4)} = \ddot{x}_i^{(4)}\left(x_i^{(4)}\right)$$

Step 4–Compute k_4:

$$k_4' = x_i^{(4)} + \Delta t\,\dot{x}_i^{(4)}$$
$$k_4'' = \dot{x}_i^{(4)} + \Delta t\,\ddot{x}_i^{(4)}$$

Step 5–Compute the new position and velocity:

$$x_{i+1}^{(1)} = x_i^{(1)} + \frac{\Delta t}{6}\left(k_1' + 2\,k_2' + 2\,k_3' + k_4'\right)$$

$$\dot{x}_{i+1}^{(1)} = \dot{x}_i^{(1)} + \frac{\Delta t}{6}\left(k_1'' + 2\,k_2'' + 2\,k_3'' + k_4''\right)$$

Error Estimation

A computer simulation method could be developed using the lower-order and less precise Euler method already described. However, it will be seen that more precise, higher order methods are required because of the effect of roundoff error and truncation error on numerical integration. Truncation error is caused because we are not integrating the differential equations of motion exactly. If we choose the timestep Δt to be too large, the method will not be sufficiently precise for the requisite precision of the problem. These errors will accumulate as the simulation proceeds. If we choose the timestep Δt to be too small, the precision problem is overcome but errors accumulate nonetheless due to a growth in error in terms below those of our start precision. These smaller errors will, in sum, grow as the simulation proceeds and will eventually render the results meaningless. This is roundoff error.

In the simulation of the miraculous movement of the sun in the ecliptic plane, there are two principal periods where an error analysis is required. The first is when the sun moves when the prophet Isaiah asks God to fulfill the request of Hezekiah to cause the sun' shadow to recline 10° on the dial of Ahaz. The second part of the simulation is when the sun occupies its new position in the ecliptic and the earth-moon barycenter moves under the influence of the fixed sun.

An error analysis can be conducted for the Runge-Kutta integration methods in the form:

$$\varepsilon \ = \Gamma\,\Delta t^5 + O\left(\Delta t^6\right)$$

where ε is the truncation error per timestep in the numerical integration for the 4th-order Runge-Kutta method and Γ are the lumped terms of the truncated Taylor expansion. We can assume that Γ is constant. Let y_{n+1}^* be the exact answer after one timestep Δt. We compare the relative error of two timesteps; in the first case the answer is obtained by choosing a $\Delta t = \Delta t_1$ and a (more accurate) approach is selected by dividing the Δt into two parts where $\Delta t_2 = \Delta t/2$. Each yields approximate results which are $y_{n+1,1}$ and $y_{n+1,2}$ respectively. Using the Richardson extrapolation method[1] it can be shown that:

$$y^*_{n+1} - y_{n+1,1} = \Gamma\,\Delta t^5 \frac{x_{n+1} - x_n}{\Delta t_1}$$

$$y^*_{n+1} - y_{n+1,2} = \Gamma\,\Delta t^5 \frac{x_{n+1} - x_n}{\Delta t_2}$$

where x_{n+1}-x_n is the difference between the two values over which one is integrating at the beginning and end of the timestep. We choose the position to be this term and this term varies approximately 0.9 A. U. per 90 days (about ¼ of one complete orbit). For 1-day timesteps this yields a value of approximately 0.01 for the right-hand side of these equations. After manipulation of these equations, they yield,

$$\varepsilon = \Gamma\,\Delta t^5 \approx \frac{320}{3\Delta t}\left(y_{n+1,2} - y_{n+1,1}\right)$$

In the first part of the simulation, when the sun is moved, the timestep Δt is of the order of 0.01 days. A timestep of 1 day was chosen thereafter. Numerical experiments showed that by running cases where the time step Δt was set to half day. The difference was found to be less than 10^{-8} A. U. per timestep. Assuming, conservatively, the error is 10^{-8} A. U. per timestep the accumulated error over one complete orbit will be approximately three decimal places in the units of the last decimal place of desired precision (namely 10^{-8} A. U.) yielding a net precision of 10^{-6}. The same number of timesteps were used for the period when the sun moved. The sun movement was tested in the range of 0.1-0.2 A. U. The net result is that the accumulated error during this period is less than for the 1-day timesteps.

Elsewhere in the appendices, in the discussion of the calculation of the perihelion passage, it is shown that the earth-moon barycenter can vary by as much as 4.7×10^6 m or 5 decimal place accuracy in astronomical units (A. U.). Hence obtaining higher precision than that obtained from using the 4th-order Runge-Kutta simulation is not justified since the simplifying assumption of the earth-moon barycenter to represent the separate and perturbed motion of the earth and moon is greater than the error caused by the numerical approximation.

Finally, the problem of roundoff error for the numerical integration of orbits is discussed by Brouwer and Clemence. They showed that for the general numerical integration of the second order differential equations of orbital motion the error after n timesteps is $0.1124n^{3/2}$ in the units of the last decimal place of the desired precision. The growth of roundoff error results in only orbits of short duration being confidently modeled for high precision problem. For 1-day time steps for a problem requiring a 360-day orbit simulation then eight decimal place accuracy is required to obtain five decimal place accuracy at the end of the simulation. This is greater than the error expected from this simulation but, as the authors point out, this theory is general and is a guide rather than a rule.

Example

To emphasize the points made in the preceding theoretical discussion, we will compare the results of a Keplerian, exact solution of the circular orbit (360-day year) of the earth-moon barycenter around the sun to those obtained using 4th-order Runge-Kutta. The start conditions are:

$$x_i^{(1)} = 0.99040487,\ y_i^{(1)} = 0.0$$
$$\dot{x}_i^{(1)} = 0.0,\ \dot{y}_i^{(1)} = 0.017285229$$

After a 1 day, the new orbital position and velocity is:

$$x_{i+1}^{(1)} = 0.99025404,\ y_{i+1}^{(1)} = 0.017284352$$
$$\dot{x}_{i+1}^{(1)} = -0.00030166\ \dot{y}_{i+1}^{(1)} = 0.017282597$$

A numerical integration using the 4th-order Runge-Kutta computer program used in this study yielded the following result after a 1-day timestep:

$$x_{i+1}^{(1)} = 0.990254036,\ y_{i+1}^{(1)} = 0.0172843515$$
$$\dot{x}_{i+1}^{(1)} = -0.00030166\ \dot{y}_{i+1}^{(1)} = 0.017282597$$

The results show that, using 1-day timesteps yields an acceptable truncation error in this case. While this is only a sample the results are consistent with what one expects from the error analysis.

Reference

1. Brouwer, D., Clemence, G. M.: *Methods of Celestial Mechanics*, New York & London: Academic Press, 1961.

APPENDIX 'I'
NUMERICAL SIMULATION OF THE SUN'S MIRACULOUS REVERSAL OF APPARENT MOTION

Numerous numerical experiments were conducted to establish whether the hypothesis of the miraculous event of the sun's shadow reversing on the sundial of Ahaz was a true reversal of the sun's apparent path in the sky. Such a fantastic event should be amenable to a physical treatment which, in turn, could be seen to be in harmony with the events described in the Bible. It will be shown that this is indeed the case.

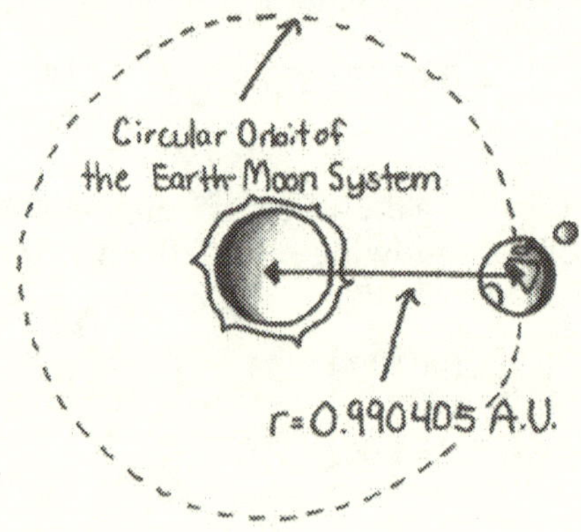

As previously noted, a Divine cause is set by the word of the Bible. It is treated as truth with nothing added or subtracted. The Holy Scriptures provides the substance of these facts and we are left to interpret the true meaning. The problems of celestial motion are primarily what physicists and mathematicians refer to as *initial value problems* and rigorous start conditions are required to solve the differential equations of motion with precision. Inaccuracy or error in computation results when the initial conditions are incompletely or inaccurately described. We will use the Bible to provide the necessary initial conditions. Further errors are introduced if the approximation used is insufficient to provide the necessary precision. Their values were determined using the following exegetic and logistical reasoning:

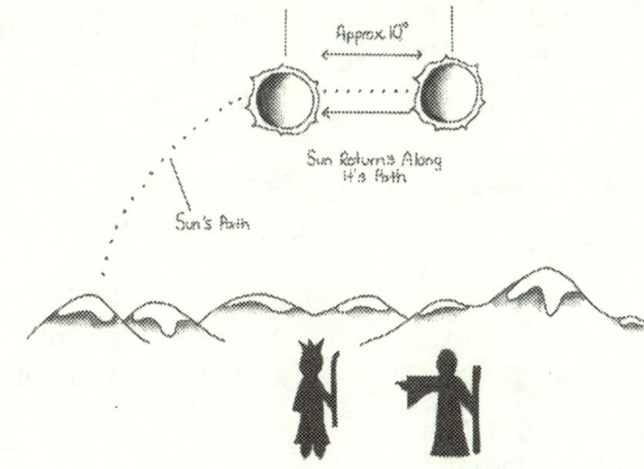

The sun is described as returning on an apparent path in the sky from which it came. ***"And Isaiah the prophet cried unto the LORD: and he brought the shadow ten degrees backward, by which it had gone down in the dial of Ahaz"*** 2 Kings 20:11. This is interpreted to mean that the sun returned, to a high degree of precision, on its apparent path across the sky in the horizon view of Isaiah the prophet and King Hezekiah. We now know that the apparent path of the sun is caused primarily by the daily rotation of the earth on its rotational axis (refer to the chapter on astronomical time for a complete description). The movement of the sun is actually along the *ecliptic*, the plane on which the planetary orbits of the Solar System approximately inhabit. Ancient people would not have understood how to interpret this miraculous event. It is proposed that this is the reason why the ancients would have been greatly confused by the relatively small but significant changes in the lunar month and solar year that resulted. It would require ancient astronomers to find other ways to model the apparent motion of celestial objects and adjust their calendar. By employing the principles of modern astronomy and celestial mechanics we can completely describe and model these observable phenomena as a movement of the sun in the ecliptic plane. This miraculous event would cause all of the planets in the solar system to shift their original orbits in the ecliptic plane due to the large changes in the central, solar gravitational forces that would result. Motion of the sun other than in the ecliptic plane is not possible as the resultant gravitational forces would throw all solar system objects into non-planar orbits. Further, non-planar movement of the sun would violate the proper meaning of the biblical description. This motion explains why the moon and the earth both apparently changed their cyclic periods from 30 days to 29½ days and 360 days to 365¼ days respectively. The moon and the earth would be affected differently by God's movement of the sun in the ecliptic plane as their position and relative velocity with respect to the sun would be different.

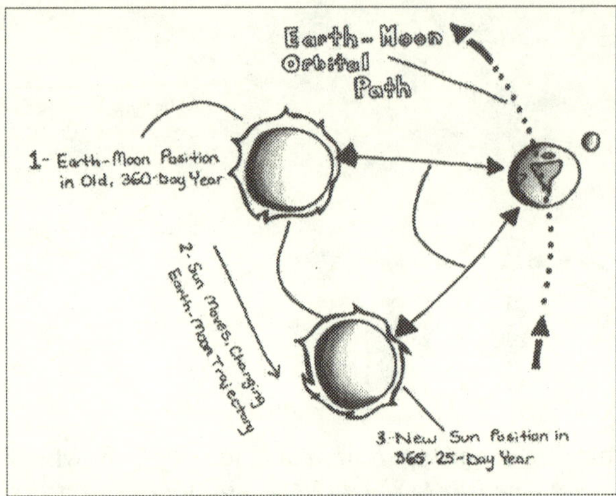

The initial conditions are further restricted by the requirement that the shadow on the dial reverse itself by the prescribed amount of 10° on the sundial of Ahaz. This restricts the allowable magnitude of the sun's movement.

The direction of the reversal of the sundial's shadow further restricts the apparent motion of the sun in the ecliptic to be in the same direction as the counter-clockwise motion of the earth's orbit. Further, the movement would have to occur over a short period of time relative to the period of a day to fit the description and to prevent the rotation of the earth on its axis from negating the sun's movement. An interesting option is implied in Isaiah's offer for the sun to go forward or backward: ***"And Isaiah said, This sign shalt thou have of the LORD, that the LORD will do the thing that he hath spoken: shall the shadow go forward ten degrees, or go back ten degrees?"*** 2 Kings 20:9. Had Hezekiah chosen for the shadow to go forward, the motion of the Sun would be in the opposite direction in the ecliptic plane. It is interesting to contemplate how the resulting time shift that would result would signify Hezekiah's additional fifteen years of life,

The Scriptures and the historical records of so many ancient civilizations point to a 360-day year with 12 months of 30 days each (Genesis 7). The Bible record implies (from the ancient practice of keeping equinoctial feasts at the spring and autumn equinoxes on the same 15th day of the month) and historical evidence (from the astronomical records of equal numbers of days between subsequent equinoxes) supports an original, circular orbit of the Earth around the Sun (ellipticity = 0). This sets the magnitude and direction of the radius and velocity vectors values required to uniquely define the initial value problem in the numerical simulation where,

$$x = 0.990405AU, y = 0AU$$

$$\dot{x} = 0, \dot{y} = 0.0172852AU / day$$

A law of Kepler (mathematically formalized by Newton) requires the conservation of angular momentum as a first approximation of the earth's orbit to a high degree of precision (the unperturbed orbit). In vector mathematics, this yields,

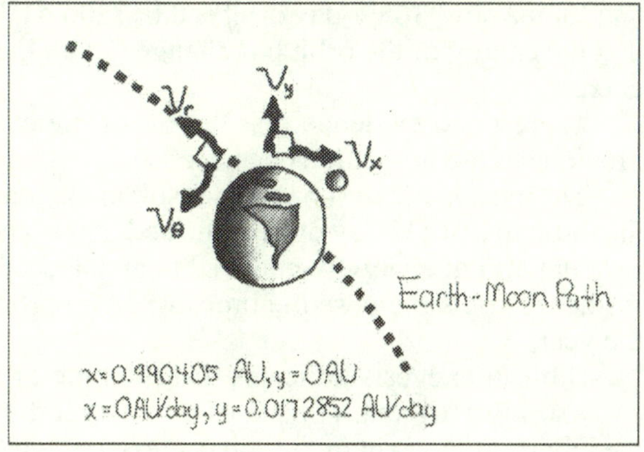

$$\vec{h}\hat{k} = \vec{r} \times \vec{v}$$

Where r is the radius (position) vector and v is the relative velocity vector. Kepler's 3rd law shows how the square of the period is proportional to the 3rd power of the semi-major axis of the orbit,

$$P^2 \alpha a^3$$

This reduces the equation to,

$$h\hat{k} = a\hat{i} + v_v \hat{j}$$

at the instant when the earth is at perihelion where a is the magnitude of the semi-major axis and v_y is the velocity component normal to the position vector (i,j,k) are the unit vectors for a positive, right-handed coordinate system. For orientation, the *unit vector k* points normal to the ecliptic. The semi-major axis changes with orbital size and these equations show directly that the constant orbital torque increases with an orbital transfer from a 360-day year to a 365-¼ day year. This requires that, if we approximate the movement of the sun to occur at an instant in time, the separation distance of the earth and sun must increase in order to obtain the requisite transfer. This condition also restricts the range of motion of the sun. The value of h for the old, circular orbit 360-day orbit is 0.017120 AU^2/day

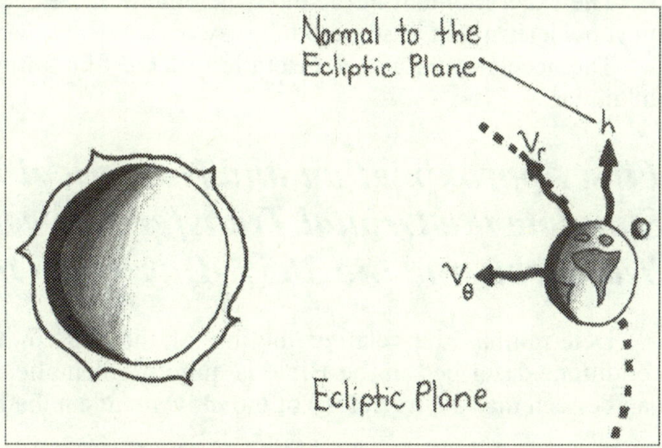

and for the new, 365¼-day orbit is 0.017200 AU^2/day. These values also imply that the energy of the orbit has changed, with the 365¼-day orbit having more energy,

There is no evidence that the tilt of the earth was changed immediately previous to the miraculous occurrence.

The motion of the sun would result in the transferal of the earth from a 360-day orbit to a 365¼-day orbit at the end of the sun's motion in the ecliptic. Any residual orbital energy would lead to an unacceptable, orbital instability. This further restricts the possible times when an orbital transfer occurs throughout the year,

Biblical exegesis indicates that the time of the year was in late winter or early spring. Although this does not restrict the range of possible times when the Divine movement of the sun occurred, it is a good way to check the validity of the results. The numerical simulation will reveal the time in the new, 365 ¼-day year calendar by allowing computation, in ephemeris time, of the time from the earth-moon perihelion passage.

There are several factors that not known *a priori* and experiments must necessarily be devised to determine them.

The sundial of Ahaz is never described. We have some idea from archaeological evidence of the types of dials used in those days. Further, it would appear that the dial was based on a pattern taken from a sacrificial alter King Ahaz observed in Damascus: ***"And king Ahaz went to Damascus to meet Tiglathpileser king of Assyria, and saw an altar that was at Damascus: and king Ahaz sent to Urijah the priest the fashion of the altar, and the pattern of it, according to all the workmanship thereof. And Urijah the priest built an altar according to all that king Ahaz had sent from Damascus: so Urijah the priest made it against king Ahaz came from Damascus"*** 2 Kings 16:10-11.

The trajectory of the Sun is unknown. Theoretically, any number of trajectories could be chosen to yield the same effect of having the sun return on its original course. The restrictions are set by the conditions stated above,

The exact moment in the day when the miracle occurred is unknown and must be determined in some other way.

The acceleration and deceleration of the Sun's motion in the ecliptic is unknown.

First Approximation and Numerical Integration to Simulate the Orbital Transfer between the 360-Day Year Orbit and the 365¼-Day Year Orbit

Determining the relative motion of the Sun in the ecliptic to fit the conditions described in the Bible is quite problematic. From the diagram, it can be seen that the trajectory of the movement can be bounded but relatively large degrees of freedom remain. Further we do not know what the velocity vector of the Earth's relative motion is. Nor can we be sure of the effect of the perturbation of the Sun's relative position will have on the Earth.

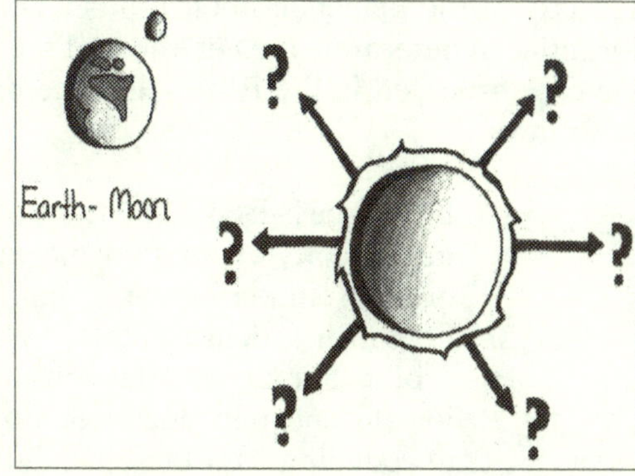

The approach taken to handle the great uncertainty of this problem is resolved in a twofold way:

By making the approximation that the orbital transfer was instantaneous, we can use exact, analytical methods to reduce the range of possible transfer criteria. This method allows us to eliminate immediately a large number of options. We will call this approach a *first approximation* to ensure it is understood that it does not constitute the final (correct) solution,

A *numerical integration* using an as yet to be described method was used to accurately model the orbital transfer from the 360-Day orbit to the 365¼-day orbit. The results of the first approximation were refined in the numerical integration routine (which allowed for a finite period of time for the Sun to move).

First Approximation – Minimization Formulation

The minimization of a residual error in the search for a problem solution is referred to as a minimization problem. They are distinguished by a priori limitations on the allowed values of independent variables. Those limitations are set by Scripture and known physical limitations. These problems are of the sort,

$$\varepsilon = \lim_{j \to \infty} \left| \delta_{j+1} - \delta_j \right|; j = 1,2,3,...$$

where δ is the solution of interest and j represents the jth attempt at determining a solution. ε is the error with the objective to minimize ε. The assumption in the use of this approach is that the change in position of the sun is instantaneous. It is obvious that this is not correct but represents an adequate first approximation. We must guess at certain features of the old orbit and test hypotheses concerning it. Fortunately, we know the current characteristics of the present, 365¼-day orbit with great precision. The method for determining orbital elements for the 365¼ day orbit in 713/2 B. C. are described elsewhere in the appendix. We validate our approach based on the already described principle of Divine Cause-Natural Effect. This principle states that the movement of the sun out of its original position in the old orbit was miraculous. This is the Divine Cause. However, the Natural Effect is the change in the gravitational forces whose influence changed the position and velocity of the planets in their orbits. This allows us to use existing physical formulae to determine the net effect of the sun's movement in accordance with the case as stated in the Bible. For the present case, the procedure proceeds as follows:

1. Using the 2-Body equations of motion, determine the position and the velocity vectors for the earth-moon barycenter for half of the orbit (from perihelion to aphelion),
2. Establish a possible total velocity value(s) which occur in both orbits. For an instantaneous transfer of the sun's position between its old and new location, no other location is possible without introducing an orbital instability,
3. Determine the position vector of the old to new sun position and calculate the horizon angle (it should be reasonably close to 10°),
4. Validate the assumption using a numerical simulation of the result.

An Example Calculation of the Instantaneous Orbital Transfer Approximation

The best way to illustrate the principle is to demonstrate using an example. The earth-moon barycentric system (E-M) is considered to be orbiting the sun in various possible orbits of unknown ellipticity. Our biblical and historical studies indicate that this orbit was undoubtedly circular but we also investigated elliptical-elliptical orbital transfers as well. We devise an x,y graphical reference frame broken up into four quadrants as seen in the diagram. In our reference frame of looking down on the ecliptic – the plane in which the sun and the E-M are contained–we are looking from approximately the North Celestial Pole. The E-M moves around the sun in a counter-clockwise rotation, as does the earth's rotation on its own axis. This forms what is commonly referred to as a right-hand positive rotation. To understand what this means, take your right hand and place all of your fingers together with your thumb pointing up. Move your fingers in the direction of the rotation. Note how the thumb continues to point upwards. If the rotation were in the opposite direction–clockwise–the thumb would point downwards. We say the thumb pointing up is a positive rotation, the thumb pointing down would be a negative rotation. Note the 'E' and 'W' denoting "East" and "West." The sun appears to rise in the east because it is the place on the earth's surface that moves from the shadow of night first. This location moves counter-clockwise and eventually moves back into the shadows. In order for the sun to make the shadow return on Ahaz's dial, the sun must move into quadrants three or four and cannot move into one or two. This would have been the case had Hezekiah selected the shadow to go forward on the dial rather than return on the dial. The diagram shows the range of possible locations of the sun's movement from its original position in the old orbit. The biblical record places further restrictions on the range of possible movement that we will describe below.

Next, we must determine the possible velocity values at each position and ephemeris time for each orbit. The starting point for each is the perihelion and the ending point is the aphelion. The starting epoch is time zero and the ending point is exactly half the sidereal year. Note that this is an astronomical calculation so the tropical year is not used.

The units of the study were in astronomical units (AU) for position and AU/Day for velocity. An astronomical unit is defined by the International Astronomical Union (IAU) as being exactly $1.49597870 \times 10^{11}$ m. The equations set out by Taff[4] were used to determine the position and velocity. They are:

Step 1–The orbital ephemeris time epoch is set. In our example, we choose t = 90 days,

Step 2–The orbital period (n) is determined in rads/day. The value is determined from Kepler's 3rd law,

$$n = \frac{2\pi}{P}$$

Where P is the period we are considering. For the present, sidereal year it is $365^d.25636042 + 1^d.1 \times 10^{-7}\, T_E$ where T_E is measured in Julian Centuries (of 36,525 days) from Jan. $0^d.5$, 1900 E. T.

Step 3–The mean anomaly of the position is determined using the formula,

$$M = nT$$

The mean anomaly after 90 days is,

$$M = 2 \times 3.14159265 \div 365.25636 \times 90 = 1.5481912 \text{ rads} = 88°.704822$$

Step 4-The mean anomaly can then be converted into the eccentric anomaly using Kepler's equation,

$$E_n = E_o - \frac{(E_0 - e \sin E_0 - M)}{1 - e \cos E_0}$$

(and employing Newton's false-root, or, *regula falsi* method). A value of E_0 is guessed at and E_n is computed. One possible initial guess is to set E_0=M. If E_n is different than E_0, the new value for E_0 is E_n and the calculation is attempted again until the results are equivalent to within a certain tolerance. For this study, we reduced the errors to the eighth decimal place.[7] The eccentricity e was set using the ancient value determined by a calculation proposed by Meeus[1] (see elsewhere in the appendix) where e = 0.01775698. The final value for the eccentric anomaly is E = 1.565948 rads = 89°.722211.

Step 5–The distance of the E-M to the sun can be computed using the equation,

$$r = a(1 - e\cos E)$$

In this case, r = 1 × [1 - 0.01775698 × cos (89°.722211)] = 0.9999139 AU

Step 6–The true anomaly can be calculated using the formula,

$$v = \cos^{-1}\frac{\cos E - e}{1 - e\cos E}$$

The true anomaly is the actual angle of the E-M position relative to they x,y coordinate system. In this case, it is

v = cos[-1] [(cos(89°.722211) – 0.01775698) ÷ (1 – 0.01775698 × cos(89°.722211))] = 1.583706 rads = 90°.73967

Step 7–The x and y location can now easily be determined from the set,

$$x = r\cos v$$

$$y = r\sin v$$

For us, x = 0.9999139 × cos(90°.73967) = -0.012909 AU and y = 0.9999139 × sin(90°.73967) = 0.999831 AU.

The calculation of the x and y values allow us to compare our results to the position determined by the numerical simulator.

7 The expected, minimum required precision was 5-6 decimal places in distance in astronomical units (AU). The additional 2 decimal places were to account for round-off error. Round-off error in numerical integration is discussed elsewhere in the appendix.

Step 8-It remains to compute the x and y components of the velocity vector. They are computed from the equations,

$$v_x = \frac{-na \sin v}{\sqrt{1-e^2}}$$

$$v_y = \frac{-na(e + \cos v)}{\sqrt{1-e^2}}$$

In this case, v_x = -0.017203 AU/day and v_y = 0.000083 AU/day.

The same procedure for any elliptical orbit can be taken so this was done for both old and new orbits. It was found that this calculation was used over and over again so it was programmed on a computer. An interesting–and important–observation is that the time of the year corresponds to a specific (x, y) and (v_x, v_y) value. If we know the moment when the E-M is at perihelion on the calendar and add 90 days to it, we can determine the exact moment when an event occurs using this calculation. The calendar time for E-M perihelion crossing was determined by Meeus[1] and is presented elsewhere in the appendices.

The point in ephemeris time when the old and new orbits have the same magnitude in velocity were determined using the equation,

$$|v_{o,n}| = \sqrt{v_{xo,n}^2 + v_{yo,n}^2}$$

where o,n represents either old or new orbits. Note that the ephemeris time difference from the time of perihelion passage in both orbits can be quite different. The required angle to obtain the correct velocity components of either the new orbit or the old orbit was determined using vector mathematics. The transformation is applied to the velocity of the components of one orbit to see if the velocity components of the other orbit can be reproduced. It is not always possible to obtain an answer using this method. The angle obtained is the angle of the sun's movement necessary to cause the orbital transfer. This angle is directly related to the angle of the sun's shadow change on the dial of Ahaz.

A program was written in the Visual Basic language for the Microsoft® Excel™ spreadsheet software. The basis for the numerical routine was extracted from *Numerical Recipes.*[3] The program was tested by successfully duplicating a circular orbit. A further test is to have the body return to the same position after exactly one year. Errors in the dimension of astronomical units (AU) no greater than 10^{-8} were tolerated. The results were further validated by comparison to analytical solutions for certain cases. In all cases, the program was found to agree with the analytical solutions within the expected range of accuracy.

Once the instantaneous transfer cases were run and a possible solution was determined, the same run was validated and adjusted using the numerical integration program. The program performed the following tasks:

The start position and velocity vectors for a particular time of year in the 360-day orbit were set,

The sun was moved along a prescribed, straight trajectory. The distance traveled was traversed at a velocity of 90% of *c*, light speed (tests were run to vary this velocity with insignificant differences in the final results),

A numerical integration of the equations of motion was conducted using the 4th order Runge-Kutta method until the earth-moon (E-M) barycenter point returned to the same orbital true anomaly.

In many runs the E-M did not return to the same point after the completion of one year (a complete orbit). This represented an orbital instability, meaning this case was incorrect and required adjustment (or possibly rejection) as a possible solution.

Since only one complete orbit was required (and no more than two), automatic time-step adjustment was not used. Instead, precision checking was obtained by doubling the number of timesteps for each orbit.

The orbital transfer from a circular orbit with 360-days was obtained by moving the sun approximately 10° in the ecliptic. This remarkable fact is a confirmation of the biblical record. The final results are as follows.

Time, Position and Velocity at the Time of Transfer in the 360-Day Orbit

Initial location: x = 0.100266 AU, y = 0.985317 AU
Initial velocity: v_x = -0.017196 AU/day, v_y = 0.004984 AU/day
Rot Angle = 10°.948, e = 0, a = 0.990405 AU, t = $84^d4^h37^m$

The value of the matching total velocity was 0.0172854 AU/day. This ensures that the orbital transfer is stable.

Orbital Elements and Initial Time, Position and Velocity in the New, 365 ¼-Day Orbit

a = 1, e = 0.017757, t = $74^d7^h30^m$
M = 1.278338, E = 1.295426
r = 0.995172 AU, v = 1.312556 rads

Initial location: x = 0.23770 AU, y = 0.96242 AU
Initial velocity: v_x = -0.0168 AU/day, v_y = 0.00408 AU/day
Ephemeris time from perihelion passage = $74^d7^h30^m$
Where the starting point (x_0, y_0) is the coordinates of the perihelion (the

point of closest approach of the Sun the E-M barycenter). The perihelion passage in calendar time was calculated through a formula provided by Meeus[1] provided elsewhere in the appendix. These are the orbital coordinates for the instant of the beginning of the 365-¼ day year. Therefore, it *is* possible to have a 360-day year, move the sun approximately 10° in arc (as observed from earth) and reproduce a new, stable 365¼ -day orbit, just as the Bible states. The reader is reminded that the reasons for the actual orbit was slightly greater than ten is described in Chapter 3.

Further, Meeus' calculations (outlined in another part of the appendix) for the estimated E-M perihelion passage for the year 714 B. C. was Nov. $26^{d}2^{h}$. Advancing $74^{d}7^{h}$ yields Feb. 10th, 713 B.C. as the day when the miracle occurred. Two warnings, however, in this calculation must be considered. This date fits well with the expected season for Sennacherib's assault on Jerusalem.

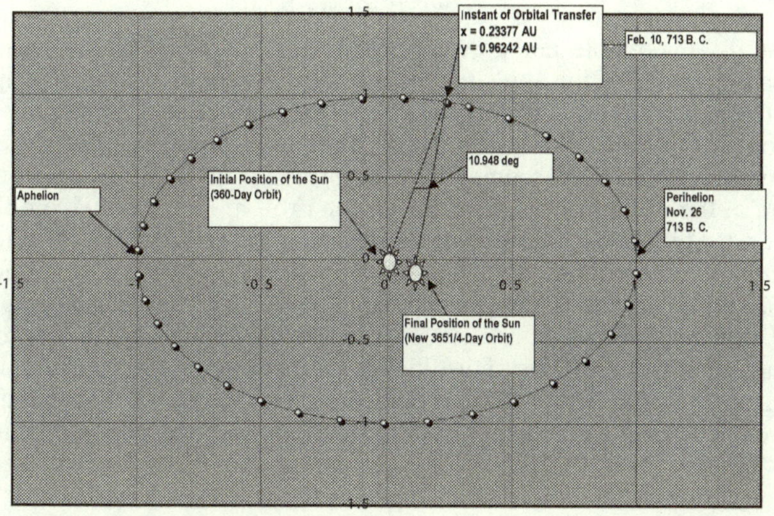

Non-Zero Ellipticity of the Original 360-Day Year Orbit

A question that may arise from the preceding question is: "What about a non-zero ellipticity of the original, 360-day year orbit? Is this possible?" The preceding discussion has assumed that the original orbit was circular and not elliptical, as the present orbit is. The answer we shall find is, yes, it is possible that the original orbit had a non-zero ellipticity. Previous evidence presented in Chapter 4 from the ancient astronomical records of civilizations pre-dating the eighth century B. C. point to an equal number of days from equinox to equinox. This provides substantial support for a circular, zero-ellipticity, 360-day year orbit.

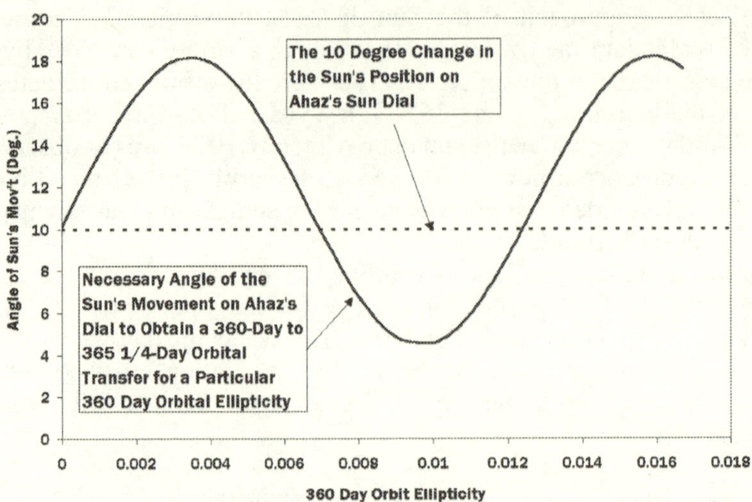

A study of possible non-zero ellipticities was undertaken to investigate the possible angles of the sun's movement to allow for an elliptical-elliptical orbital transfer from the old to new orbit. The graph shows the approximate conditions for this orbital transfer. It is important to emphasize that this study is approximate in that it assumes that the orbital transfer was instantaneous and that, at the instant of orbital transfer, the orbit motion can be completely described by two-body, Newtonian equations of orbital motion. Numerical simulation has shown that this is not quite as discussed above. Nevertheless, it will be sufficiently accurate for the present purposes. The dashed line shows the 10° change in the sun's relative position in the ecliptic at the time of the sun's movement. Where the sinusoidal curve varies from this dashed line, it is increasingly unlikely that this is a possible solution. We have seen that Sun movement angles greater than 1° from the Bible's stated 10° is unsuitable. Larger 360-day orbital eccentricities (on the graph, the right hand side of the graph) are also unlikely as they make the year less uniform in time from equinox to equinox. It would appear there is indeed a low eccentricity orbit at e = 0.0075 that might be a possible exception to assuming that the pre-eighth century B. C., 360-day year orbital eccentricity was zero. Nevertheless, this eccentricity is so low that presuming that this older orbit was zero is still the best approximation we can use based on the limited data about the orbit that we possess.

References:

1. Meeus, J.: *Astronomical Formulae for Calculators*, 4th Ed. Richmond, VA: Wilmann-Bell Inc., 1988.
2. Brouwer, D., Clemence, G. M.: *Methods of Celestial Mechanics*, New York & London: Academic Press 1961.
3. *Numerical Recipes in FORTRAN 77: The Art of Scientific Computing*, Cambridge: Cambridge University Press, 1986.

APPENDIX 'J'
SOLAR RADIATION BEFORE AND AFTER THE ORBITAL TRANSFER

At the instant of orbital transfer–when the earth moved from its older 360-day orbit to one of 365-¼ days–the separation distance with the sun would be identical for both orbits. Solar radiation at this point in time would be the same and so no climactic changes would occur. However, over the year, the new elliptical orbit would result in some differences in the amount of heat captured in the earth's atmosphere and at the surface. In this appendix we will discuss those changes.

Date	I_t/I_o
January 1	1.0335
February 1	1.0288
March 1	1.01733
April 1	1.0009
May 1	0.9841
June 1	0.9714
July 1	0.9666
August 1	0.9709
September 1	0.9828
October 1	0.9995
November 1	1.0164
December 1	1.0288

De Jong[1] states there are six factors that effect the amount of solar radiation reaching the Earth:

1. The solar constant,
2. The latitude and longitude of the point on the earth and the time of the year,
3. The atmosphere,
4. The albedo of the Earth's surface,
5. The elevation of the location,
6. The time unit.

The amount of energy retained at the earth's surface and the atmosphere can be assumed to be approximately the same throughout the ages.[8] The "solar constant" I_0 is the intensity of solar radiation reaching the earth at the mean sun-earth separation distance. This distance is the same as *the astronomical unit* (A. U.), the measurement unit commonly used in astronomy and in this book. The units of I_0 are cal/cm²/sec. The value of I_0 has been calculated at 1.979-2.02 cal/cm²/sec. Robinson[2] shows that this energy can be computed from the formula:

$$E_0 = \pi r_0^2 I_0$$

where r_0 is the mean radius of the Earth and E_0 is the power intercepted by the earth.

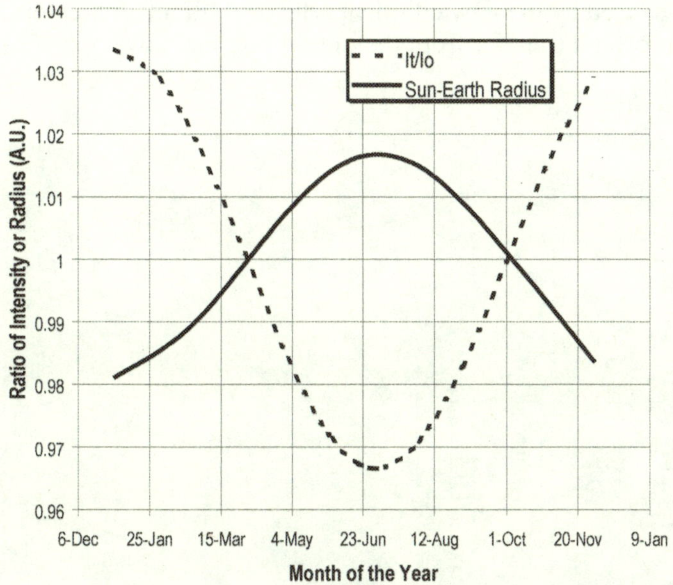

The Sun emits 3.85×10^{23} kW of energy and the Earth receives 1.79×10^{14} kW. Robinson tabulates the relative intensity of the solar radiation throughout the year by creating the solar radiation intensity I_t as a ratio of the mean solar radiation intensity ("the solar constant") I_0:

It can be seen that the earth receives more of the sun's energy in January (summer in the southern hemisphere) than in July (summer in the northern hemisphere). This is because the earth is in aphelion in January (closest to the

8 An argument might be made that the amount of atmospheric particles has increased since ancient times due to industrialization. This may, in turn, affect other atmospheric factors that will affect the amount of heat.

sun) and in perihelion in July (furthest from the sun). The maximum difference in intensity from the mean is 3.35% at aphelion.

We stated previously that for the older 360-day year the orbit was circular with a radius of 0.9904 A. U. The solar radiation intensity in the older year was constant throughout the year. The earth at this time was more uniformly heated. However, the earth would still have experienced her seasons as now due to the earth's tilt affecting the incidence of the sun's rays on a particular position on the earth.

The difference in mean distance of the earth-sun of 0.4% can be related directly to the intensity of solar radiation. Hence, the difference in intensity between the old 360-day year and the new 365¼-day year from the sun has diminished by 0.4%. To put this in context, the difference in intensity of the sun's energy between the northern and southern hemispheres in their respective summer months is, at present, as much as 7%. Therefore, the fluctuations of solar energy caused by the new elliptical orbit are still much greater than those caused by the orbital transfer from the old orbit to the new.

References

1. De Jong, B.: *Net Radiation Received by a Horizontal Surface at the Earth*, Delft: Delft University Press, 1973.
2. Robinson, N.: *Solar Radiation*, New York: Elsevier Publishing Company, 1966.

APPENDIX 'K'
DATING THE 4TH OF JEHOIAKIM, KING OF JUDAH AND THE ACCESSION YEAR OF NEBUCHADNEZZAR, KING OF BABYLON

A comprehensive discussion of this matter is provided by Jones[1] and the reader is referred to his work for a complete analysis. Rather than attempt to duplicate his work or build the case for the chronology of events, we will simply state the chronology:

Crown Prince Nebuchadnezzar Attacks The Regions Near Judah (606 B.C.) – Historical analysis reveals that Nebuchadnezzar was enlisted by his father, King Nabopolassar, to lead the army in war against the remnant of Assyria and the allies of Assyria, particularly, Egypt. Nabopolassar had revolted against Assyrian domination and near the end of his reign and his son Nebuchadnezzar destroyed the remnants of the Assyrian empire and assimilated the territories held by them, including Judah, Syria and Samaria. At this time some of the royal house of Judah was taken captive. This is the period when Daniel was taken captive:

"*In the third year of the reign of Jehoiakim king of Judah came Nebuchadnezzar king of*
Babylon unto Jerusalem, and besieged it." (Dan. 1:1)

Further support for the idea that there were captives taken from Judah in the 3rd year of Jehoiakim is provided by Josephus. He quotes the Babylonian historian Berosus who describes Nebuchadnezzar's return to Babylon after the death of his father, Nabopolassar, as having to deal with the issue of "…the captive Jews…"[2]. This must mean, of course, that some Jews were already captive before Nebuchadnezzar began his accession year.

To further support this idea, we note that Daniel and his fellow captives were to be trained for three years before appearing before the king:

"*And the king appointed them a daily provision of the king's meat, and of the wine which he drank: so nourishing them three years, that at the end thereof they might stand before the king.*" (Daniel 1:5)

Daniel stands before King Nebuchadnezzar in the second year of his reign (Dan. 2:1). This would fit if the first year of Daniel's training was in the last year of Nabopolassar, the second year was the accession year of Nebuchadnezzar and the third year was the first year of Nebuchadnezzar's reign.

This fits with the narrative of the Babylonian Chronicle, listed in the main body of the book.

Nabopolassar, King of Babylon Dies, Nebuchadnezzar Ascends the Throne in His Ascension Year, Nebuchadnezzar Fights the Battle of Carchemish (605 B.C)

The Babylonian Chronicle records that Nabopolassar died in the month Ab (the fifth month) on the eighth day. That would be July/August in our modern calendar. The Chronicle further states that Nebuchadnezzar was crowned king on the first day of the month Elul (the sixth month) or August/September in our modern calendar. Thus the autumn of 605 B.C. and the winter/spring of 604 B.C. would be Nebuchadnezzar's accession year (again, recorded in the Babylonian Chronicle) and so this does not count as the beginning of his regnal years. That begins on Nisan (March/April) of 604 B.C.

The prophet Jeremiah speaks of this period in connection with Nebuchadnezzar twice:

"*The word that came to Jeremiah concerning all the people of Judah in the fourth year of Jehoiakim the son of Josiah king of Judah, that was the first year of Nebuchadrezzar king of Babylon.*" (Jer. 25:1)

Jeremiah's "first" year in Jeremiah 25:1 refers to Nebuchadnezzar's accession year. The Hebrew phrase "first year" is "hashshanah haroshniyth". This is the only occurrence of this phrase in the Old Testament and can be alternately translated the "beginning year" or year of accession, as argued by Finegan and Tadmore.[3,4]

"*Against Egypt, against the army of Pharaohnecho king of Egypt, which was by the river Euphrates in Carchemish, which Nebuchadrezzar king of Babylon smote in the fourth year of Jehoiakim the son of Josiah king of Judah.*" (Jer. 46:2)

In parallel, the Babylonian Chronicle refers to Nebuchadnezzar fighting Pharaoh Necho at Carchemish prior to ascending the throne in Babylon.

Jeremiah 46:2 dates this as the same time as Jehoiakim's fourth regnal year. Other investigators commonly support the date of the Battle of Carchemish as 605 B.C.

Nebuchadnezzar First Regnal Year (604 B.C)

From the foregoing, Nebuchadnezzar's first regnal year (according to Babylonian rules for dating the times of the reigns of kings) begins on Nisan 1, 604 B.C.

This then connects Nebuchadnezzar's early reign to the fourth year of Jehoiakim's reign.

The Reigns of Jehoiachin and Zedekiah

Finally, it is worth noting in passing that we have leapt over the reigns of Jehoiachin and Zedekiah. The scriptural references to the reigns of Jehoiachin and Jehoiakim are as follows. In keeping with our trend of going backwards in time, Jehoiachin's reign is described first, and then the earlier reign of Jehoiakim:

"*Jehoiachin was eight years old when he began to reign, and he reigned three months*

and ten days in Jerusalem: and he did that which was evil in the sight of the LORD. And when the year was expired, king Nebuchadnezzar sent, and brought him to Babylon, with the goodly vessels of the house of the LORD, and made Zedekiah his brother king over Judah and Jerusalem." (2 Chr. 36:9,10)

This connects Jehoiachin and Zedechiah. So Zedekiah reigned eleven years and Jehoiachin reigned three years and ten days. Now Jehoiakim:

"*Jehoiakim was twenty and five years old when he began to reign; and he reigned eleven years in Jerusalem. And his mother's name was Zebudah, the daughter of Pedaiah of Rumah.*" (2 Ki. 23:36)

And so Jehoiakim's reign was for eleven years. The diagram shows the reigns of the Nebuchadnezzar and the reigns of these kings.

Note that king Jehoiachin is carried away in captivity in Nebuchadnezzar's eighth year of his reign:

"*And Jehoiachin the king of Judah went out to the king of Babylon, he, and his mother, and his servants, and his princes, and his officers: and the king of Babylon took him in the eighth year of his reign.*" (2 Ki. 24:12)

The reader is referred back to the main body of the text, showing how Ezekiel's prophecies "pins" these dates down, leaving no room for error.

References:

1. Jones, F. N. *Chronology of the Old Testament: A Return to Basics*. 15th Ed., Green, AR: Master Books, Inc., 2004.
2. Josephus, Flavius: *Antiquities*, Book 10, Part 11, 1, Michigan: 1999.
3. Finegan, J. *Handbook of Biblical Chronology*. Peabody, Mass: Hendrickson Publishers, 1998.
4. Tadmor, H."Chronology of the Last Kings of Judah". *Journal of Near Eastern Studies*, Vol. 15, Chicago: The University of Chicago Press, 1956.

APPENDIX 'L'
THE ECLIPSE AT BUR-SAGALE

Claudius Ptolemy's *Almagest* contains over eighty solar, lunar and planetary positions.[1] Chronologists often use the *Almagest* to create their chronologies of historical events. Eclipse records are very valuable because they are relatively rare astronomical events. Armed with the modern methods of mathematics and physics, these recorded events can be reproduced with good precision. As mentioned elsewhere in the appendices, eclipses have the added benefit of being locally observable. That means that even though there might be an eclipse observed in the United States, it is likely such an eclipse would not be observed in, say, the Middle East because of a difference in longitude. The eclipse's unique attributes make it well-suited for dating work.

The first observation in the *Almagest* is a solar eclipse at Bur-Sagale. Many chronologists have dated this solar eclipse as occurring on June 15, 763 B.C. Our thesis is that one cannot use astronomical observations–like eclipses–to date historical events prior to 713 B.C. because events prior to this date must use the orbital characteristics of a 360-day year. This must mean that the date for this eclipse is wrong. To be clear, this does not mean that the eclipse was not observed. The event is recorded in the Assyrian Eponym List and was undoubtedly correct. It is only the calendar date that is in question.

The work of physicist Robert Newton verifies this assertion. Newton was interested in trying to improve the physical models of changes to the earth's rotation and orbit by examining ancient astronomical observations.[9] His research led him to a detailed examination of the *Almagest*. Newton found disparities between Ptolemy's recorded observations and his numerical simulations of orbital motion. He published a controversial book that claimed that Ptolemy's work was fraudulent.[2] Some of Newton's claims were challenged and he was accused of being over-zealous in his criticisms.[3] An examination of these arguments is beyond the scope of this book. Newton found that he could not verify any of the observations in the *Almagest* prior to 600 B.C. Similarly, Newton investigated the Venus tablets of Ammizaduga, king of Babylon, in the eighteenth century B.C. He asserts that no chronological events could be accurately dated using these observations[4].

---

9 Specifically, Newton wanted to examine the differences between ephemeris time (E.T.) and universal time (U.T.). Ephemeris time is a time system based on mathematical models of celestial motion and universal time is used as a basis of civil timekeeping.

Of interest to us is that Newton found the *Almagest's* dating of events after 600 B.C. was generally reliable for dating and correct to within the time precision of hours or days. Astronomical observations after the seventh century B.C. using a modern understanding of celestial motion would be a correct application and is an important validation of the findings of the book.

Lastly, the dating of the solar eclipse of Bur-Sagale has been alternately recommended to be either June 24, 791 B.C. or June 13, 809 B.C.[5] These dates are at odds with Josephus. Therefore, the June 15, 763 B.C. date used by many chronologists for the solar eclipse of Bur-Sagale is not reasonably supported and selecting this date for the eclipse is a matter of interpretation.

Our position is that any attempt at developing a chronology based on astronomical observations prior to the seventh century B.C. will always be wrong. This is because it presumes that the current earth orbit of 365 ¼ days has always occurred and we have shown that this is not the case. Our contention is that once the 360-day year principle is accepted, dating of astronomical events prior to the seventh century B.C. will allow accurate dating.

References

1. Jones, F. N. *Chronology of the Old Testament: A Return to Basics*. 15th Ed., Green, AR: Master Books, Inc., 2004.
2. Newton, R. R. *The Crime of Cladius Ptolemy*, Baltimore: The Johns Hopkins University Press 1977.
3. See, for example, Gingerich, O. "The Trouble With Ptolemy," ISIS, Vol. 93, pp. 70-4, 2002.
4. Newton, R. R. *Ancient Planetary Observations and the Validity of Ephemeris Time*. Baltimore: The Johns Hopkins University Press, 1976.
5. Thiele, E. R. *The Mysterious Numbers of the Hebrew Kings*. Grand Rapids, MI: Zondervan, 1983.

Glossary

Abib–The oldest name used to mark the beginning of the Jewish year. It is sometimes referred to as the "opening of the year" and occurs in the months of March or April of our present calendar. Later, in the fifth century B. C., when the Jews returned to their land after 70 years of exile in Babylon, they adopted the Babylonish calendar and this month was renamed Nisan.

Albedo–The fraction of incident light reflected by the earth's surface

Analytical Solution–The exact solution of an equation.

Angles Only–A method for determining the location and trajectory of celestial bodies by measuring only their angles relative to some measurement reference frame.

Aphelion--The point in the orbit of a planet around the sun when the planet is farthest from the sun.

Astrolabe–An astronomical instrument used prior to the invention of the telescope.

Astronomical Unit (A. U.)–An astronomic dimension used to measure the distance between celestial bodies. This unit was originally designated as the average distance between the earth and the sun and later formalized by astronomers to the exact distance of 149,600,000 km.

Axis–The line which joins the north and south poles of the celestial sphere.

Barycenter–The location in space of the center of mass for two or more orbiting celestial bodies. In celestial mechanics, the location of the barycenter is more important than a physical location as Newton's laws showed that the true point of an orbital center is its center of mass and not necessarily its apparent physical location. An example of this principle is used in the simulation methods used in this book. The earth and moon are separate bodies that orbit the sun but the earth-moon barycenter is the center of mass whose position can be used to represent the location of the earth (to a particular degree of precision).

Component–The portion of a vector whereby the vector's magnitude and direction are related to a spatial reference frame. For example, in this book, a velocity vector is resolved in the Euclidean x, y and z reference frame. The velocity vector can then be expressed in terms of the x, y and z directions of this reference frame.

Cycle–An interval of time when a closing and opening epoch are coincidental. The time event most commonly observed is the recurrence of the appearance of a moon phase (for the Jews, the recurrence of the New Moon) or the recurrence of the equinox (when the Sun is observed to be directly east and when the period of day and night are equal). Modern astronomy has much more exact methods based on the modern knowledge that the earth and moon revolve around the sun.

Diurnal–Recurring daily.

Eccentric–The deviation from a circular path. Astronomers measure eccentricity by a number varying between zero (no deviation from a circular orbit) to one (a theoretical orbit which is so elliptical that it is a straight line).

Ecliptic–Formally, the great circle of the celestial sphere that is the apparent path of the sun or the earth with respect to the sun. The ecliptic forms a plane that the planets of the solar system's orbits closely trace.

Ellipse–An oval. Formally, a closed, planar curve created by the sum of the distance between any two fixed points is a constant. The orbital trace of planets in the solar system.

Ephemeris Time–A uniform time system defined by the equations of motion for the planets.

Epoch–An instant or point in time. In time measurement, there are two sets of events: the opening and closing epochs of the time event and the coincidental opening and closing measured events. A time measurement occurs when the measured event is described in the reference frame of the time event.

Equinox–The epoch when the day and night are of equal time and when the sun is in the eastern direction. Astronomically, the equinox occurs when the equator is aligned with the ecliptic. In the modern calendar, the equinox occurs around March 22nd (the vernal equinox) and September 23rd (the autumnal equinox).

Ethanim–The oldest name used to mark the ending of the Jewish year. It is sometimes referred to as the "closing of the year" and occurs in the months of September or March of our present calendar. Later, in the fifth century B. C., when the Jews returned to their land after 70 years of exile in Babylon, they adopted the Babylonish calendar and this month was renamed Tisri.

Firmament–The arch of the sky over the head of the observer. The firmament is the horizon perspective that is always used in the Bible.

Foci–Plural of focus, in particular, the location of the sun in the elliptical orbit of the earth and earth-moon barycenter.

Force–The acceleration of a mass at rest. In orbital motion, these forces are caused by gravity.

Gnomon–The part of the sundial which casts the shadow.

Heliocentric System–The sun is in the center. This system is inferior to the barycentric system as it is known that the sun actually orbits around the barycenter of the solar system due to the mutual gravitation of the planets. See barycenter.

Hezekiah–A king of the Southern Kingdom of Judah between 725 B. C. and 686 B. C. His father was King Ahaz and his son was King Manasseh. He received a sign from God whereby the sun's shadow returned on a sundial erected by his father Ahaz 10°.

Horizon–The approximate flat surface where the earth and the sky meet. Astronomers have more exact definitions not discussed in this book.

Intercalate–The insertion of days into a calendar. Intercalary periods are introduced to align measured events, such as the occurrence of opening or closing of a year, with a time events (such as the recurrence of the solar equinox).

Israel– (1) The name of a man, formerly named Jacob, who was renamed by God (Genesis 32:28), (2) The name of a people who descended from the man Israel, formed as a nation at their Exodus from the land of Egypt, (3) A territory east of the Great Sea (now the Mediterranean Sea), south of Syria, north of Sinai and west of the Arabian desert, (4) After the revolt of Jeroboam (1 Kings 11:31, 1 Kings 12:19,20), the ten tribes occupying their inherited lands north of Jerusalem and excluding the tribe of Judah (sometimes called the "Northern Kingdom").

Judah–(1) A man, one of the sons of Jacob (later named Israel) (Genesis 29:35), (2) A territory which included Jerusalem and sometimes called the "Southern Kingdom" after the revolt of Jeroboam.

Lunisolar–Pertaining to the sun and moon. In particular, lunisolar transformations refer to the cycles of the moon and the sun and their relation to each other.

Mean–An average obtained by determining the middle between two extremes.

Meridian–A great circle of the celestial sphere that passes through both poles and a particular place. The prime meridian is the place on earth

Momentum–The property of a moving body which describes its action under a constant force.
where the zeroth longitude is designated and passes through Greenwich, England.

Moon Phase–An observed change in the Moon's appearance caused by the shadow of the earth. Typical phases are the New Moon (Moon completely in shadow), the Crescent Moon (Moon ¼ and ¾ in shadow), the Half Moon (Moon ½ in shadow) and the Full Moon (no shadow).

Nadir–The point on the celestial sphere directly opposite the Zenith and directly below the observer on earth.

Naked Eye Astronomy–Astronomical methods used without aid of the telescope or other modern observational tools; the methods used by ancient astronomers can collectively be described by this term.

Nisan–The name of the opening month of the Jewish calendar after the Jews returned from exile in Babylon. See Abib.

North Celestial Pole–The northerly direction of the celestial sphere.

Numerical Integration–An approximate mathematical method to integrate integrable variables. Typically, as in this book, the integration cannot be performed in any other known way. The precision and accuracy of the method is dependent on the approach used.

Orbit–A path of one celestial body revolving around another. Orbits are said to be either closed or open. A closed orbit means that the celestial body returns to the same position in space after a period of time. An open orbit is one in which the body does not return to the same position.

Perihelion–The point in the orbit of a planet around the sun when the planet is closest to the sun.

Planetary Aberration—The mutual gravitational effect on the orbit of solar system planets due to the (changing) location of other masses in the solar system other than the sun.

Point Mass–A theoretical consideration used by physicists where the total mass of an object is considered to occur at one point in space. In this book, the mass of the earth and the moon are considered to occur at one point in space; their center of mass. The approach is insufficient in some cases. For example, it is known that in high precision modeling of the moon's motion, the slightly non-spherical form of the earth must be taken into account.

Precession of the Equinoxes–The westward motion of the equinoctial points due to the coupled effect of solar system gravitational attraction and the non-spherical distribution of mass on the earth. The effect can be duplicated with a child's spinning top. When the spin is constant the top's axis remains fixed. If the spin is not constant, the axis begins to wobble and precess.

Radius–The separation distance between two points.

Rectify–To remedy or set right. In calendars it refers to the adjustment of time periods to account for differences between observed time events and the constant periods measured by a calendar.

Semi-Major Axis–In an elliptical orbit, ½ the width of the elongated (longest) distance between two points on the oval. The semi-major axis is half the distance between the aphelion to the perihelion.

Solstice–The shortest and longest periods of light during the year. In the northern hemisphere this occurs at December 22nd and June 22nd respectively.

Sundial–Any device that measures the progress of the sun's shadow to determine time. Sundials typically have hour angles which divide the day into (somewhat) equal units of time.

Synodic Period–Formally, the period between two consecutive conjunctions of the moon. A synodic period is more generally the time period between the appearance of two moon phases (ex. Full Moon to Full Moon, New Moon to New Moon, etc.).

Time–A measured period of events. A time period is described by an opening and closing epoch. Time periods are expected to be continuous, repeatable and observable.

Tisri–The name of the closing month of the Jewish calendar after the Jews returned from exile in Babylon. See Ethanim.

Universal Time–Time which is based on Greenwich Time (i. e. at the prime meridian).

Vector–Any quantity that has both a magnitude and a dimension. For example, velocity (speed) is a vector as it pertains to a body that is moving in a particular direction at a certain rate. However, distance is not a vector because although it has a magnitude (ex. 1 mile) it does not have any direction in particular.

Watch–The ancient method for dividing the day and night into equal parts. The watch preceded the introduction of the hour. There were either three or four watches for day or night depending on the Jewish era.

Yahweh–A name of God. It means "He who shall be."

Zenith–The point on the celestial sphere directly opposite the nadir and directly above the observer on earth.

www.ingramcontent.com/pod-product-compliance
Lightning Source LLC
LaVergne TN
LVHW091001080826
845145LV00003B/1080

* 9 7 8 1 5 9 9 3 2 0 1 3 7 *